Ordnance Survey

Cycle

23 one-day routes in

The Peak District

Compiled by
Gordon Selway

PHILIP'S

TOURS

Contents

Acknowledgments
AA Photo Library back cover, 41, 47, 52, 60, 64, 82, 128 • Derek Forss 19, 34, 39, 71, 77, 83, 88/89, 109, 122, 132 • Judy Todd 94, 101, 107, 115
• edited by Melissa Arnison-Newgass • designed by James Hughes
• picture research by Jenny Faithfull • production by Claudette Morris

Back cover photograph: Monsal Dale

First published 1996 by

Ordnance Survey   and   Philip's, an imprint of
Romsey Road   Reed Books
Maybush   Michelin House
Southampton   81 Fulham Road
SO16 4GU   London SW3 6RB

Text and compilation
Copyright © Reed International Books Ltd 1996
Maps Copyright © Crown Copyright 1996
First edition 1996

A catalogue record for this atlas is available from the
British Library

ISBN 0 600 58880 0
(Ordnance Survey ISBN 0 319 00773 1)

Printed in Spain

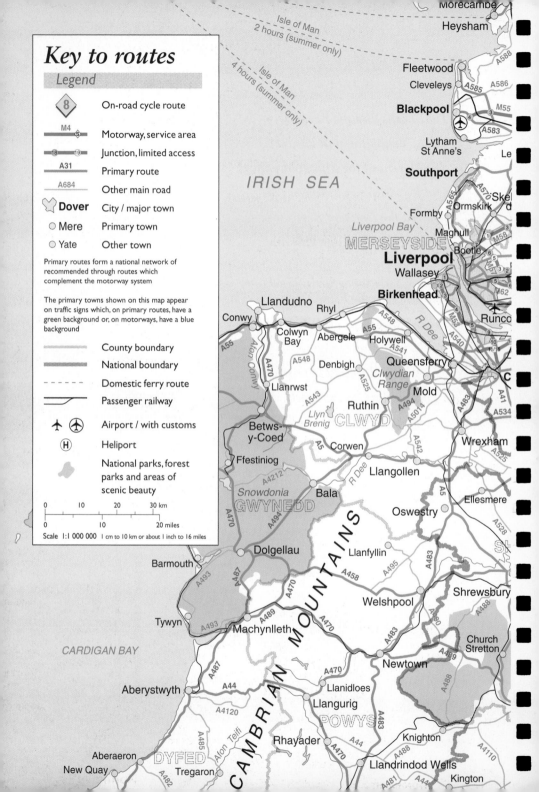

Key to routes

Legend

◇ 8	On-road cycle route
M4 Ⓢ	Motorway, service area
18 19	Junction, limited access
A31	Primary route
A684	Other main road
Dover	City / major town
◎ Mere	Primary town
○ Yate	Other town

Primary routes form a national network of recommended through routes which complement the motorway system

The primary towns shown on this map appear on traffic signs which, on primary routes, have a green background or, on motorways, have a blue background

	County boundary
	National boundary
– – – – –	Domestic ferry route
	Passenger railway
✈ Ⓧ	Airport / with customs
Ⓗ	Heliport
	National parks, forest parks and areas of scenic beauty

Scale 1:1 000 000   1 cm to 10 km or about 1 inch to 16 miles

0   10   20   30 km
0   10   20 miles

IRISH SEA

Isle of Man 2 hours (summer only)
Isle of Man 4 hours (summer only)

Morecambe
Heysham
Fleetwood   A588
Cleveleys   A585   A586
Blackpool   M55
Lytham   A583
St Anne's
Le

Southport   A570   Skel   d

Formby   Ormskirk
Liverpool Bay   Maghull   M58
MERSEYSIDE   Bootle
Liverpool
Wallasey
Birkenhead   M53   Runco

Llandudno   Rhyl   A548   R Dee   A540
Conwy   A55   Runco
Colwyn   Abergele   A55   Holywell   A541
Bay   A548   Queensferry   C
A55   Denbigh   Clwydian   Mold   A41
Llanrwst   A525   Range   A5014   A534
Betws-   A543   Ruthin   A494
y-Coed   Llyn   CLWYD   Wrexham
Ffestiniog   Brenig   A542   A525
A4212   Corwen   R Dee   Llangollen   A5   Ellesmere
Snowdonia   Bala   Oswestry   A528
GWYNEDD   A5   St
Dolgellau   Llanfyllin   A483
Barmouth   A493   A487   A458   A495   Shrewsbury
A470   Welshpool   A490   A488
Tywyn   A493   A489   A470   Church
Machynlleth   A483   Stretton
CARDIGAN BAY   A489   Newtown   A489
A487   A470   A488
Aberystwyth   A44   Llanidloes   POWYS
A4120   Llangurig   A483
A487   CAMBRIAN MOUNTAINS   A470   Knighton
A485   Rhayader   A44   Llandrindod Wells   A4110
Aberaeron   DYFED   Afon Teifi   A470   A488
New Quay   Tregaron   A482   A481   A44   Kington

Quick reference chart

Route	Page	Distance (kilometres)	Grade (easy/moderate/strenuous)	Links with other routes[1]	Tourist information centres[2]
On-road routes					
1 Kedleston, Ashbourne and Hungry Bentley	18	50	▨▨	13,14	Ashbourne 01335 343666
2 The Churnet Valley and Somersal Herbert	24	57	▨▨	14	Ashbourne 01335 343666
3 Staffordshire Moorlands	30	49	▨▨▨	4,5,13, 14,15	Leek 01538 381000
4 The Cloud and the Caldon Canal	36	40	▨▨	3	Leek 01538 381000
5 The Goyt Valley and Macclesfield Forest	40	50	▨▨▨▨	3,15	Macclesfield 01625 504114
6 Winnats and Tideswell	46	55	▨▨▨▨	15,17, 18	Castleton 01433 620679
7 Last of the Summer Wine	52	58	▨▨▨		Holmfirth 01484 687603
8 Loxley Valley	60	38	▨▨▨▨	19	Sheffield 0114 2734671
9 Burbage, Eyam and Froggatt	64	50	▨▨▨	16,17, 18	Sheffield 0114 2734671
10 Between Chesterfield and Bakewell	70	48	▨▨▨▨	21,22	Chesterfield 01246 207777
11 From Cromford, visiting industrial sites and quiet countryside	76	34	▨▨▨	12,22	Amber Valley 01773 841488
12 Two Trails and the Barmote	82	60	▨	11,13, 14,20	Matlock 01629 55082
13 Ilam, Hartington and Parwich	88	54	▨▨▨	1,3,12, 14	Ashbourne 01335 343666
14 The Dove and the Manifold valleys	94	56	▨▨	1,3, 12,13	Leek 01538 381000

[1]**Links with other routes** Use this information to create a more strenuous ride or if you are planning to do more than one ride in a day or on a weekend or over a few days.The rides do not necessarily join: there may be a distance of up to five kilometres between the closest points. Several rides are in pairs, sharing the same starting point, which may be a good place to base yourself for a weekend.

[2]**Tourist Information Centres** You can contact them for details about accommodation. If they cannot help, there are many books that recommend places to stay. If nothing is listed for the place where you want to stay, try phoning the post office or the pub in the village to see if they can suggest somewhere.

Peak District

*T*his book covers the area bounded by Derby, Stoke, Manchester, Huddersfield and Sheffield. It includes the Peak National Park – the first to be designated under the National Parks and Countryside Act of 1949. The most visited national park in England and Wales, it is within two hours travel of most people in England.

The Peak is hilly but not mountainous: the highest point on Kinder Scout is only 640 m (2088 ft). The middle is the White Peak, an area of widely mined, carboniferous limestone. The millstone grit of the High Peak (or Dark Peak) embraces the White Peak on three sides, although mainly to the north. The many dry valleys in the White Peak contain few rivers while extensive bogs are characteristic of the uplands in the High Peak where valleys contain strings of reservoirs.

The Peak is a wonderful region to explore by bike. There is an abundance of quiet country lanes, old turnpikes and drovers' routes superseded by today's motor roads. Old railways made into trails for walkers, riders and cyclists offer easy, mostly uninterrupted, routes. It is difficult to find routes without hills, however, the trails – engineered for steam – are often easier cycling than the parallel roads.

These routes are designed to explore the Peak and let the cyclist get to know the area and so often the routes are not quite as direct as they might be simply in order to include some interesting features. Some routes overlap; you may join parts of two or more routes to give further variety. The weather in the Peak District is very variable: you should make sure that you are ready for rain, or for much colder weather than forecast, even during the summer.

Preface

Thanks are due to staff of the county and district councils, the National Trust, stately homes and country parks, and of the Peak Joint Planning Board for their time and information. I would like to thank Mrs Spencer in Uttoxeter and Mr and Mrs Isard in Sheffield for their kindness and to members of local cycle campaign groups: John Huff, Alan Moffatt, John Newson, Sally Robinson, Rosemary Sharples, John Tozer and Bob Troup for their help and suggestions

Abbreviations and instructions

Instructions are given as concisely as possible to make them easy to follow while you are cycling. Remember to read one or two instructions ahead so that you do not miss a turning. This is most likely to occur when you have to turn off a road on which you have been riding for a fairly long distance and these junctions are marked **Easy to miss** to warn you.

If there appears to be a contradiction between the instructions and what you actually see, always refer to the map. There are many reasons why over the course of a few years instructions will need updating as new roads are built and priorities and signposts change.

If giving instructions for road routes is at times difficult, doing so for off-road routes can often be almost impossible, particularly when the route passes through woodland. With few signposts and buildings by which to orientate yourself, more attention is paid to other features, such as gradient and surface. Most of these routes have been explored between late spring and early autumn and the countryside changes its appearance very dramatically in winter. If in doubt, consult your map and check your compass to see that you are heading in the right direction.

Where I have encountered mud I have mentioned it, but this may change, not only from summer to winter but also from dry to wet weather, at any time during the year. At times you may have to retrace your steps and find a road alternative.

Some routes have small sections that follow footpaths. The instructions will highlight these sections where you must get off and push your bike. You may only ride on bridleways and by-ways so be careful if you stray from the given routes.

Directions

L	left
LH	left-hand
RH	right-hand
SA	straight ahead or straight across
bear L or R	make less than a 90-degree (right-angle) turn at a fork in the road or track or at a sharp bend so that your course appears to be straight ahead; this is often written as *in effect SA*
sharp L or R turn	is more acute than 90 degrees
sharp R/L back on yourself	an almost U-turn
sharp LH/RH bend	a 90-degree bend
R then L or R	the second turning is visible then immediately L from the first
R then 1st L	the second turning may be some distance from the first; the distance may also be indicated: *R, then after 1 mile L*

Junctions

T-j	T-junction, a junction where you have to give way
X-roads	crossroads, a junction where you may or may not have to give way
offset X-roads	the four roads are not in the form of a perfect cross and you will have to turn left then right, or vice versa, to continue the route

Signs

'Placename 2'	words in quotation marks are those that appear on signposts; the numbers indicate distance in miles unless stated otherwise
NS	not signposted
trig point	a trigonometrical station

Instructions

An example of an easy instruction is:

4 At the T-j at the end of Smith Road by the White Swan PH R on Brown Street 'Greentown 2, Redville 3'.

There is more information in this instruction than you would normally need, but things do change: pubs may close down and signs may be replaced, removed or vandalized.

An example of a difficult instruction is:

8 Shortly after the brow of the hill, soon after passing a telephone box on the right next L (NS).

As you can see, there is no T-junction to halt you in your tracks, no signpost indicating where the left turn will take you, so you need to have your wits about you in order not to miss the turning.

Fact boxes

The introduction to each route includes a fact box giving useful information:

 Start

This is the suggested start point coinciding with instruction I on the map. There is no reason why you should not start at another point if you prefer.

 Distance and grade

The distance is, of course, that from the beginning to the end of the route. If you wish to shorten the ride, however, the maps enable you to do so.

The number of drinks bottles indicates the grade:

Easy
Moderate
Strenuous

Page diagrams

The on-road routes usually occupy four pages of mapping each. The page diagrams on the introductory pages show how the map pages have been laid out, how they overlap and if any inset maps have been used.

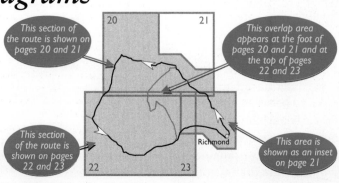

This section of the route is shown on pages 20 and 21

This overlap area appears at the foot of pages 20 and 21 and at the top of pages 22 and 23

This section of the route is shown on pages 22 and 23

This area is shown as an inset on page 21

The grade is based on the amount of climbing involved.

Remember that conditions may vary dramatically with the weather and seasons, especially along off-road sections

 Terrain

This brief description of the terrain may be read in conjunction with the cross-profile diagram at the foot of the page to help you to plan your journey.

 Nearest railway

This is the distance to the nearest station from the closest point on the route, not necessarily from the start. Before starting out you should check with British Rail for local restrictions regarding the carrying of bicycles.
(See page 15)

 Refreshments

Pubs and teashops on or near the route are listed

Before you go

Preparing yourself

Fitness
☀ Cycling uses muscles in a different way from walking or running, so if you are beginning or returning to it after a long absence you will need time to train your muscles and become accustomed to sitting on a saddle for a few hours. Build up your fitness and stamina gradually and make sure you are using a bicycle that is the right size for you and suits your needs.

Equipment
☀ Attach the following items to the bike: bell, pump, light-brackets and lights, lock-holder and lock, rack and panniers or elastic straps for securing things to the rack, map holder. Unless it is the middle of summer and the weather is guaranteed to be fine, you will need to carry extra clothes, particularly a waterproof, with you, and it is well worth investing in a rack for this purpose.

☀ Wearing a small pouch around your waist is the easiest and safest way of carrying small tools and personal equipment. The basics are: Allen keys to fit the various Allen bolts on your bike, chainlink extractor, puncture repair kit, reversible screwdriver (slot and crosshead), small adjustable spanner, spare inner tube, tyre levers (not always necessary with mountain bike tyres), coins and a phonecard for food and telephone calls, compass.

☀ Additional tools for extended touring: bottom bracket extractor, cone spanners, freewheel extractor, headset spanners, lubricant, socket spanner for pedals, spare cables, spoke-key.

Clothing
☀ What you wear when you are cycling should be comfortable, allowing you, and most especially your legs, to move freely. It should also be practical, so that it will keep you warm and dry if and when the weather changes.

☀ *Feet* You can cycle in just about any sort of footwear, but bear in mind that the chain has oil on it, so do not use your very best shoes. Leather tennis shoes or something similar, with a smooth sole to slip into the pedal and toe clip are probably adequate until you buy specialist cycling shoes, which have stiffer soles and are sometimes designed for use with specialist pedals.

☀ *Legs* Cycling shorts or padded cycling underwear worn under everyday clothing make long rides much more comfortable. Avoid tight, non-stretch trousers, which are very uncomfortable for cycling and will sap your energy, as they restrict the movement of your legs; baggy tracksuit bottoms, which can get caught in the chain and will sag around your ankles if they get wet. Almost anything else will do, though a pair of stretch leggings is probably best.

Upper body What you wear should be long enough to cover your lower back when you are leaning forward and, ideally, should have zips or buttons that you can adjust to regulate your temperature. Several thin layers are better than one thick layer.

Head A helmet may protect your head in a fall.

Wet weather A waterproof, windproof top is essential if it looks like rain. A dustbin bag would be better than nothing but obviously a breathable waterproof material is best.

Cold weather A hat that covers your ears, a scarf around your neck, a pair of warm gloves and a thermal top and bottom combined with what you would normally wear cycling should cover almost all conditions.

Night and poor light Wearing light-coloured clothes or reflective strips is almost as important as having lights on your bike. Reflective bands worn around the ankles are particularly effective in making you visible to motorists.

Preparing your bicycle

You may not be a bicycle maintenance expert, but you should make sure that your bike is roadworthy before you begin a ride.

If you are planning to ride in soft, off-road conditions, fit fat, knobbly tyres. If you are using the bike around town or on a road route, fit narrower, smoother tyres.

Check the tyres for punctures or damage and repair or replace if necessary or if you are in any doubt. Keep tyres inflated hard (recommended pressures are on the side wall of the tyre) for mainly on-road riding. You do not need to inflate tyres as hard for off-road use; slightly softer tyres give some cushioning and get better traction in muddy conditions.

Ensure that the brakes work efficiently. Replace worn cables and brake blocks.

The bike should glide along silently. Tighten and adjust any part that is loose or rubbing against a moving part. Using a good-quality bike oil lubricate the hubs, bottom bracket, pedals where they join the cranks, chain and gear-changing mechanism from both sides. If the bike still makes grating noises, replace the bearings.

Adjust the saddle properly. The saddle height should ensure that your legs are working efficiently: too low and your knees will ache; too high and your hips will be rocking in order for your feet to reach the pedals. Some women find the average bike saddle uncomfortable because the female pelvis is a different shape from the male pelvis and needs a broader saddle for support. Some manufacturers make saddles especially for women.

Cross-profiles

The introduction to each route includes a cross-profile diagram. The blue grid indicates 1-kilometre horizontal intervals and 50-metre vertical intervals

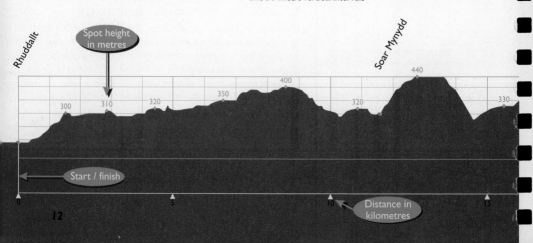

Tips for touring

The law

England and Wales have 120 000 miles of rights of way, but under the Wildlife and Countryside Act of 1968 you are allowed to cycle on only about 10 percent of them, namely on bridleways, by-ways open to all traffic (BOATs) and roads used as public paths (RUPPs).

The other 90 percent of rights of way are footpaths, where you may walk and usually push your bike, but not ride it. Local bylaws sometimes prohibit the pushing of bicycles along footpaths and although all the paths in this book have been checked, bylaws do sometimes change.

☼ You are not allowed to ride where there is no right of way. If you lose the route and find yourself in conflict with a landowner, stay calm and courteous, make a note of exactly where you are and then contact the Rights of Way Department of the local authority. It has copies of definitive maps and will take up the matter on your behalf if you are in the right.

Cycling techniques

If you are not used to cycling more than a few miles at a stretch, you may find initially that touring is tiring. There are ways of conserving your energy, however:

☼ Do not struggle in a difficult gear if you have an easier one. Let the gears help you up the hills. No matter how many gears a bike has, however, ultimately it is leg power that you need to get you up a hill. You may decide to get off and walk uphill with your bike to rest your muscles.

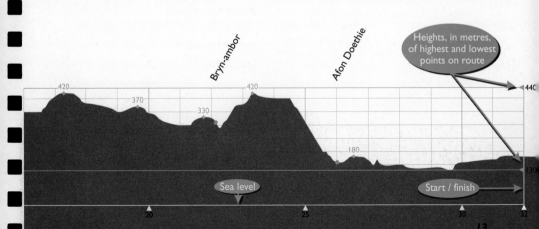

You can save a lot of energy on the road by following close behind a stronger rider in his or her slipstream, but do not try this offroad. All the routes are circular, so you can start at any point and follow the instructions until you return to it. This is useful when there is a strong wind, as you can alter the route to go into the wind at the start of the ride, when you are fresh, and have the wind behind you on the return, when you are more tired.

The main difference in technique between on-road and off-road cycling lies in getting your weight balanced correctly. When going down steep off-road sections, lower the saddle, keep the pedals level, stand up out of the saddle to let your legs absorb the bumps and keep your weight over the rear wheel. Control is paramount: keep your eyes on what lies ahead.

Traffic

The rides in this book are designed to minimize time spent on busy roads, but you will inevitably encounter some traffic. The most effective way to avoid an accident with a motor vehicle is to be highly aware of what is going on around you and to ensure that other road users are aware of you.

Ride confidently.

Indicate clearly to other road users what you intend to do, particularly when turning right. Look behind you, wait for a gap in the traffic, indicate, then turn. If you have to turn right off a busy road or on a difficult bend, pull in and wait for a gap in the traffic or go past the turning to a point where you have a clear view of the traffic in both directions, then cross and return to the turning.

Use your lights and wear reflective clothing at night and in poor light.

Do not ride two-abreast if there is a vehicle behind you. Let it pass. If it cannot easily overtake you because the road is narrow, look for a passing place or a gate entrance and pull in to let it pass.

Maintenance

Mountain bikes are generally stronger than road bikes, but any bike can suffer. To prevent damage as far as possible:

Watch out for holes and obstacles.

Clean off mud and lubricate moving parts regularly.

Replace worn parts, particularly brake blocks.

Riders also need maintenance:

Eat before you get hungry, drink before you get thirsty. Dried fruit, nuts and chocolate take up little space and provide lots of energy.

Carry a water bottle and keep it filled, especially on hot days. Tea, water and well-diluted soft drinks are the best thirst-quenchers.

Breakdowns

The most likely breakdown to occur is a puncture.

Always carry a pump.

Take a spare inner tube so that you can leave the puncture repair until later.

Make sure you know how to remove a wheel. This may require an adjustable spanner or, in many cases, no tool at all, as many bikes now have wheels with quick-release skewers that can be loosened by hand.

Security

Where you park your bike, what you lock it with and to are important in protecting it from being stolen.

Buy the best lock you can afford.

Lock your bike to something immovable in a well-lit public place.

Locking two bikes together is better than locking them individually.

Use a chain with a lock to secure the wheels and saddle to the frame. Keep a note of the frame number and other details, and insure, photograph and code the bike.

Transporting your bike

There are three ways of getting you and your bike to the start of a ride:

Cycle to the start or to a point along a route near your home.

Take the train. Always check in advance that you can take the bike on the train. Some trains allow only up to two bikes and you may need to make a reservation and pay a flat fee however long the journey. Always label your bike showing your name and destination station.

Travel by motor vehicle. You can carry the bikes:

- Inside the vehicle. With the advent of quick release mechanisms on both wheels and the seatpost, which allow a quick dismantling of the bike, it is possible to fit a bike in even quite small cars. It is unwise to stack one bike on top of another unless you have a thick blanket separating them to prevent scratching or worse damage. If you are standing them up in a van, make sure they are secured so they cannot slide around.

- On top of the vehicle. The advantages of this method are that the bikes are completely out of the way and are not resting against each other, you can get at the boot or hatch easily and the bikes do not obscure the number plate or rear lights and indicators. The disadvantages are that you use up more fuel, the car can feel uncomfortable in a crosswind and you have to be reasonably tall and strong to get the bikes on and off the roof.

- On a rack that attaches to the rear of the vehicle. The advantages are that the rack is easily and quickly assembled and disassembled, fuel consumption is better and anyone can lift the bikes on and off. The disadvantages are that you will need to invest in a separate board carrying the number plate and rear lights if they are obstructed by the bikes, you cannot easily get to the boot or hatch once the bikes have been loaded and secured, and the bikes are resting against each other so you must take care that they don't scrape off paint or damage delicate parts.

- Whichever way you carry the bikes on the outside of the vehicle, ensure that you regularly check that they are secure and that straps and fixings that hold them in place have not come loose. If you are leaving the bikes for any length of time, be sure they are secure against theft; if nothing else lock them to each other.

Legend to 1:50 000 maps

Roads and paths

Motorway

Service area (S) M 5 Elevated
Junction number 20

Motorway under construction

Trunk road
Unfenced   Footbridge
A 46 (T)

Main road
Dual carriageway
A 420

Main road under construction

Secondary road
B 4348

Narrow road with passing places
A 855   B 885

Road generally more than 4 m wide
Bridge

Road generally less than 4 m wide

Other road, drive or track

Path

Gradient: 1 in 5 and steeper, 1 in 7 to 1 in 5

Gates   Road tunnel

Passenger ferry   Vehicle ferry
Ferry P   Ferry V

Public rights of way (Not applicable to Scotland)

.... Footpath
- - - - - - - Bridleway
-·-·-·-·-·- Road used as a public footpath
-+-+-+-+-+- Byway open to all traffic

Danger Area — Firing and test ranges in the area. Danger! Observe warning notices

Tourist information

🆔 ℹ️	Information centre, all year / seasonal
P	Parking
✕	Picnic site
⚖	Viewpoint
🛆	Camp site
🚍	Caravan site
▲	Youth hostel
▨	Selected places of tourist interest
☎	Public telephone
☎	Motoring organisation telephone
⌐	Golf course or link
PC	Public convenience (in rural areas)

Railways

———	Track: multiple or single
•••••••	Track: narrow gauge
⫢⫢	Bridges, footpath
⬤┄⬤	Tunnel
⌇	Viaduct
┼┼┼┼	Freight line, siding or tramway
● a ⬤ b	Station, (a) principal, (b) closed to passengers
⊣⊢ LC	Level crossing
⫟⫟⫟⫟	Embankment
⬤┄⬤	Cutting

Rock features

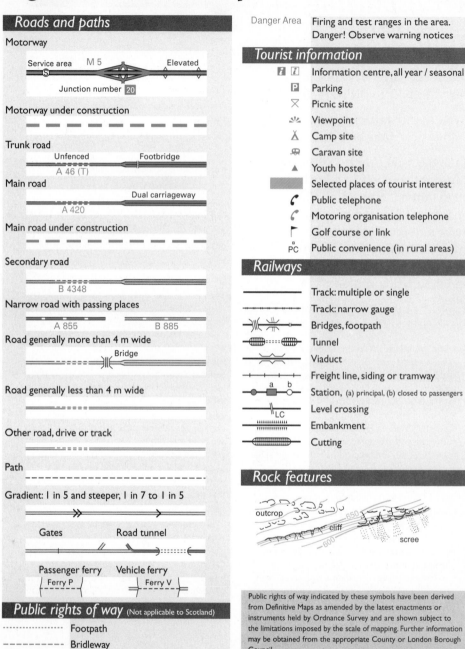

outcrop   cliff   650   600   scree

Public rights of way indicated by these symbols have been derived from Definitive Maps as amended by the latest enactments or instruments held by Ordnance Survey and are shown subject to the limitations imposed by the scale of mapping. Further information may be obtained from the appropriate County or London Borough Council

The representation on this map of any other road, track or path is no evidence of the existence of a right of way

Water features

Canal (dry)

Canal

Lake

Aqueduct

Towpath Lock

Ford

Normal tidal limit

Footbridge Bridge

Weir

Marsh or salting

Slopes

Cliff

High water mark

Flat rock

Low water mark

Lighthouse (in use)

Sand Dunes

Lighthouse (disused)

Beacon

Mud

Shingle

General features

Electricity transmission line
(with pylons spaced conventionally)

> - -> - -> Pipeline (arrow indicates direction
of flow)

ruin

Buildings

Public buildings (selected)

Bus or coach station

Coniferous wood

Non-coniferous wood

Mixed wood

Orchard

Park or ornamental grounds

Quarry

Spoil heap, refuse tip or dump

Radio or TV mast

Church or chapel with tower

Church or chapel with spire

Church or chapel without
tower or spire

Chimney or tower

Glasshouse

Graticule intersection at 5' intervals

Heliport

Triangulation pillar

Windmill with or without sails

Windpump

Boundaries

+ - + - + National

London borough

National park or forest park

NT National Trust

NT open access

NT limited access

County, region or islands area

+ + + + District

Abbreviations

P Post office

PH Public house

MS Milestone

MP Milepost

CH Clubhouse

PC Public convenience (in rural areas)

TH Town hall, guildhall or equivalent

CG Coastguard

Antiquities

VILLA Roman

Castle Non-Roman

Battlefield (with date)

Tumulus

+ Position of antiquity which cannot be
drawn to scale

Ancient monuments and historic
buildings in the care of the Secretaries
of State for the Environment, for
Scotland and for Wales and that are
open to the public

Heights

50 Contours are at 10 metres vertical
interval

·144 Heights are to the nearest metre
above mean sea level

Heights shown close to a triangulation pillar refer to the station height
at ground level and not necessarily to the summit

Kedleston, Ashbourne and Hungry Bentley

*T*his route links Derby with Ashbourne, the gateway to Dovedale and the western part of the National Park but it is also a good ride in its own right. The house and parkland at Kedleston merit a visit, but for the most part it is the countryside you pass through which is the main attraction. The site of the deserted medieval village of Hungry Bentley can be visited on summer weekends (and by arrangemet) at Bentley Fields Open Farm.

Start

Derby Station

P As above

Distance and grade

50 km (32 miles)

Easy/moderate

Terrain

Mostly lowland with short climbs on the outward section of the route including one quite steep climb out of Ashbourne over about 180 m (200 yd)

Nearest railway

Derby

Refreshments

Plenty of choice in **Derby**
Kedleston Hall Refreshment Room, **Kedleston**
Plenty of choice in **Ashbourne**
(Several pubs on route back from Ashbourne to Derby)

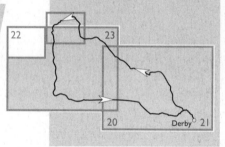

► Kedleston Park

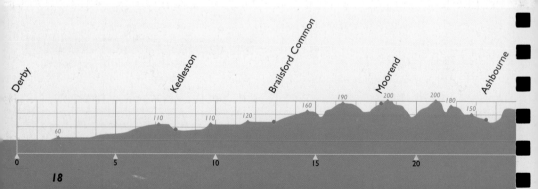

Places of interest

Derby 1

A busy city and a centre of our remaining railway industry with much of interest, often down side streets or away from the centre. The City Museum and Art Gallery has, among other things, an excellent collection of paintings by Wright 'of Derby', a magnificent collection of Crown Derby porcelain and displays about the old Midland Railway

Kedleston Hall 5

A magnificent Georgian stately home, with extensive gardens, parkland and serpentine lake. Owned by the National Trust and open to the public on most summer afternoons

Ashbourne 14

One of the gateways to the Peak at the lower end of Dovedale and the old market centre of west Derbyshire. There are many attractive buildings of the 18th and 19th centuries. On Shrove Tuesday and Ash Wednesday each year a medieval football game (with the goals several kilometres apart) is played

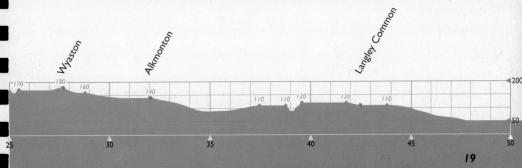

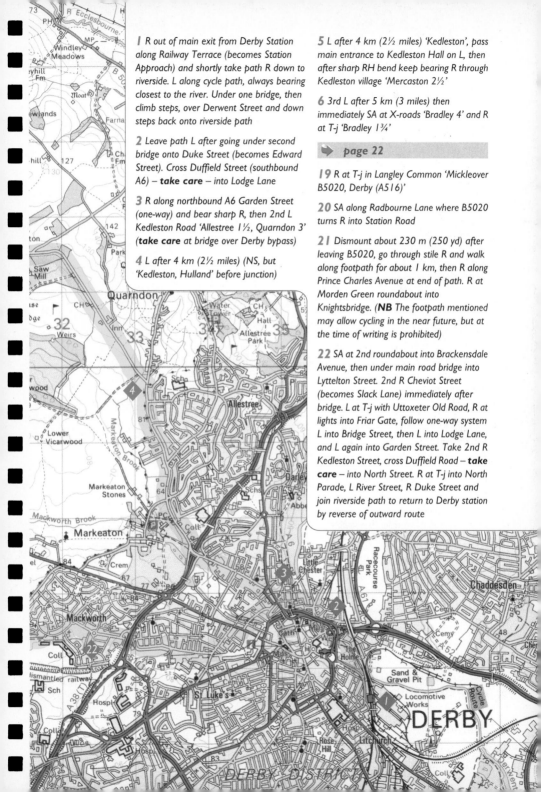

1 R out of main exit from Derby Station along Railway Terrace (becomes Station Approach) and shortly take path R down to riverside. L along cycle path, always bearing closest to the river. Under one bridge, then climb steps, over Derwent Street and down steps back onto riverside path

2 Leave path L after going under second bridge onto Duke Street (becomes Edward Street). Cross Duffield Street (southbound A6) – **take care** – into Lodge Lane

3 R along northbound A6 Garden Street (one-way) and bear sharp R, then 2nd L Kedleston Road 'Allestree 1½, Quarndon 3' (**take care** at bridge over Derby bypass)

4 L after 4 km (2½ miles) (NS, but 'Kedleston, Hulland' before junction)

5 L after 4 km (2½ miles) 'Kedleston', pass main entrance to Kedleston Hall on L, then after sharp RH bend keep bearing R through Kedleston village 'Mercaston 2½'

6 3rd L after 5 km (3 miles) then immediately SA at X-roads 'Bradley 4' and R at T-j 'Bradley 1¾'

➡ **page 22**

19 R at T-j in Langley Common 'Mickleover B5020, Derby (A516)'

20 SA along Radbourne Lane where B5020 turns R into Station Road

21 Dismount about 230 m (250 yd) after leaving B5020, go through stile R and walk along footpath for about 1 km, then R along Prince Charles Avenue at end of path. R at Morden Green roundabout into Knightsbridge. (**NB** The footpath mentioned may allow cycling in the near future, but at the time of writing is prohibited)

22 SA at 2nd roundabout into Brackensdale Avenue, then under main road bridge into Lyttelton Street. 2nd R Cheviot Street (becomes Slack Lane) immediately after bridge. L at T-j with Uttoxeter Old Road, R at lights into Friar Gate, follow one-way system L into Bridge Street, then L into Lodge Lane, and L again into Garden Street. Take 2nd R Kedleston Street, cross Duffield Road – **take care** – into North Street. R at T-j into North Parade, L River Street, R Duke Street and join riverside path to return to Derby station by reverse of outward route

7 L after 4 km (2½ miles) 'Bradley ½'

8 L (NS), then L again at T-j and shortly 1st R (in effect SA) onto Hadley Lane 'Moorend ½'

9 R at T-j after 800 m (½ mile) 'Ashbourne 2½' and immediately through Hole in the Wall

10 **Take care** – SA at X-roads with A517 'Offcote, Kniveton'

11 L at T-j 'Ashbourne 2'

12 Obliquely L at T-j with B5035 'Ashbourne'

13 Fork L 'Town Centre, Derby A52', then L again after 400 m (¼ mile) Park Road

14 R at T-j with A517 'Town Centre A52'

15 2nd L at traffic lights Old Hill (NS, one-way street) uphill past Plough PH and SA, going under Ashbourne bypass in about 1 km

16 R at T-j after 2 km (1½ miles) 'Edlaston, Wyaston'

17 R (in effect SA) between church and PH in Yeaveley

18 L in Alkmonton 'Longford, Kirk Langley' continuing along Long Lane for about 10 km (6½ miles)

 ◀ page 21

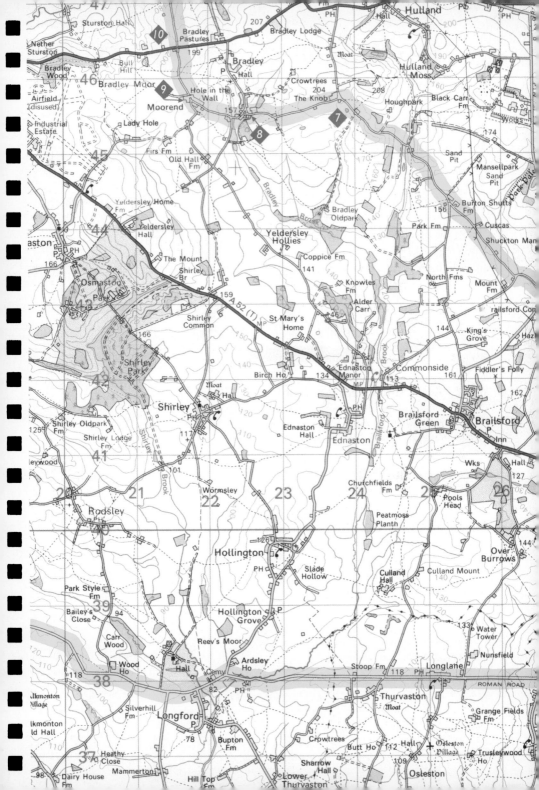

The Churnet Valley and Somersal Herbert

A day's on-road ride through the contrasting countryside south of the White Peak visiting the Churnet Valley and the uplands of southwest Derbyshire where there are extensive views in fine weather. The steep-sided, wooded valley of the River Churnet has been called Staffordshire's Switzerland and there are many enjoyable walks through the woods around Oakamoor.

Start

Johnson Monument, Uttoxeter Market Place

P Several car parks in Uttoxeter

Distance and grade

57 km (36 miles)

Easy/moderate

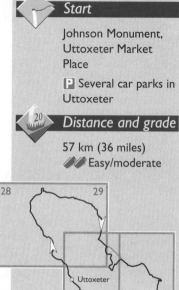

Refreshments

*Plenty of choice in **Uttoxeter***
*Pubs in **Stramshall, Hallington, Oakamoor, Ellastone** and **Roston***
*Crown Inn, **Marston Montgomery***
*Shop and PH in **Church Broughton***
*Tea room at Sudbury Hall, **Sudbury***
*Dog and Partridge PH, **Marchington***

1 Ride away from kiosk side of Johnson Memorial in Uttoxeter Market Place and fork R at roundabout by Three Tuns PH (Ashbourne B5033)

2 SA at roundabout with A50 – **take care** – busy trunk road, B5030 'Rocester, Ashbourne'

3 1st L 'Spath ¼'

➡ **page 28**

15 L at T-j (offset X-roads) after 4 km (2½ miles) 'Thurvaston 1, Marston 1, Cubley 2¾' and fork R 'Marston Montgomery ¾'

16 2nd R in Marston Montgomery (Somersal Lane, 'Somersal Herbert 2½') after Crown Inn (**Or** continue SA here and pick up directions after 4 km (2½ miles) from instruction 22)

17 **Easy to miss** – R after 2 km (1½ miles) gated road (NS) – if you pass Somersal House on left you have gone too far

18 L at T-j in Somersal Herbert 'Sudbury 2'

19 L at T-j beside chapel 'Marston Montgomery'

20 R after 800 m (½ mile) – in effect SA (NS)

➡ **page 26**

33 R in Marchington (NS) shortly after Dog & Partridge PH into Hall Lane, bear L

34 R Moisty Lane (NS)

35 R after 5 km (3 miles) at T-j with B5017 (NS) cross railway line, then 2nd L to return to Uttoxeter Market Place

Places of interest

Uttoxeter /

A modest country town with strong dairying and pastoral connections. It also has links with Samuel Johnson, compiler of the first English dictionary in the 1750s. His father sold books in the market here and Samuel refused to take his place when requested. He returned to do penance years later and the event is still commemorated each September

Alton Towers //

A spectacular, early 19th-century mansion in Tudor style (part demolished) with formal gardens. Now the grounds house one of the country's major tourist attractions, the Alton Towers leisure park. Pugin (who contributed to the Palace of Westminster) was one of a series of architects employed by the Earls of Shrewsbury to realise their dream here

Terrain

Woodland to the west of the River Dove but otherwise open country. Climbs to Hallington and past Threapwood and short climbs out of Oakamoor and leaving Somersal Herbert. A fairly long but easy ride

Nearest railway

Uttoxeter

21 R at T-j 'Sudbury 3'

22 R at T-j 'Lichfield A515, Sudbury', then immediately L 'Boylestone, Church Broughton'

23 R at T-j 'Sapperton, Church Broughton'

24 L at X-roads after I km 'Church Broughton I'

25 SA at X-roads Church Road

26 R opposite church (NS)

27 2nd R (NS)

28 L at T-j Cote Bottom Lane (NS)

29 L at T-j and L again before A564, then bear R at roundabout, cross dual carriageway bypass, R again at 2nd roundabout, and L 'Scropton' (not shown on map)

30 R at triangular T-j in Scropton 'Sudbury 2', Leathersley Lane

31 L at T-j 'Lichfield A515; Draycott-in-the-Clay 2½, King's Bromley 10'

32 R after 2 km (1½ miles) Moreton Lane 'Moreton'

 page 24

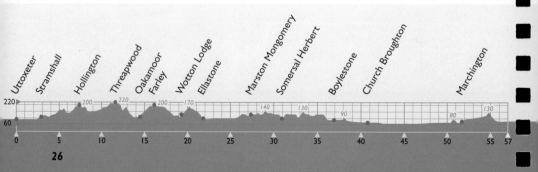

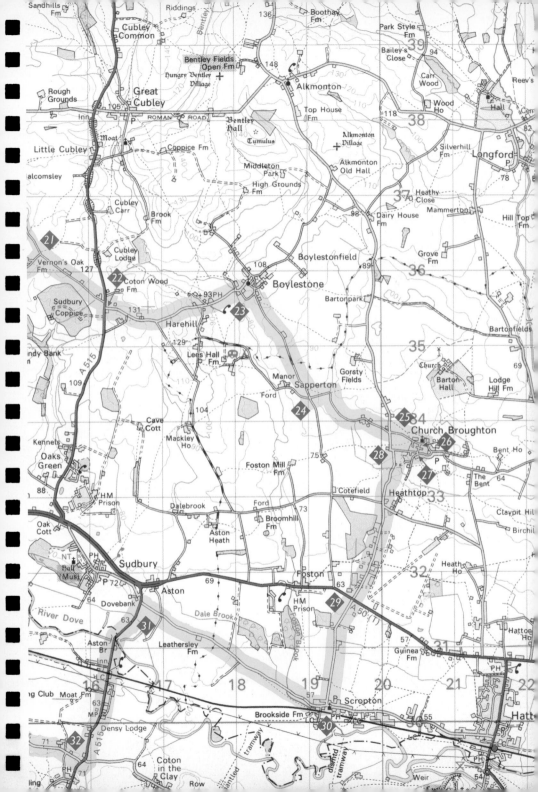

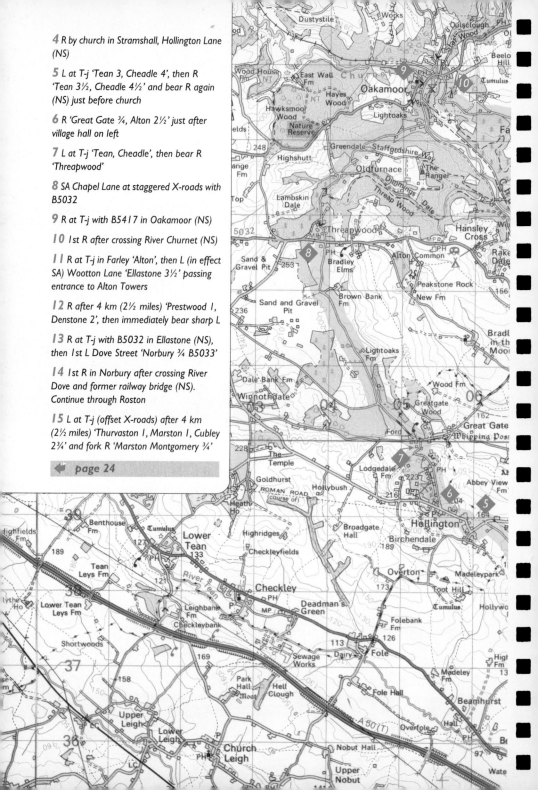

4 R by church in Stramshall, Hollington Lane (NS)

5 L at T-j 'Tean 3, Cheadle 4', then R 'Tean 3½, Cheadle 4½' and bear R again (NS) just before church

6 R 'Great Gate ¾, Alton 2½' just after village hall on left

7 L at T-j 'Tean, Cheadle', then bear R 'Threapwood'

8 SA Chapel Lane at staggered X-roads with B5032

9 R at T-j with B5417 in Oakamoor (NS)

10 1st R after crossing River Churnet (NS)

11 R at T-j in Farley 'Alton', then L (in effect SA) Wootton Lane 'Ellastone 3½' passing entrance to Alton Towers

12 R after 4 km (2½ miles) 'Prestwood 1, Denstone 2', then immediately bear sharp L

13 R at T-j with B5032 in Ellastone (NS), then 1st L Dove Street 'Norbury ¾ B5033'

14 1st R in Norbury after crossing River Dove and former railway bridge (NS). Continue through Roston

15 L at T-j (offset X-roads) after 4 km (2½ miles) 'Thurvaston 1, Marston 1, Cubley 2¾' and fork R 'Marston Montgomery ¾'

← **page 24**

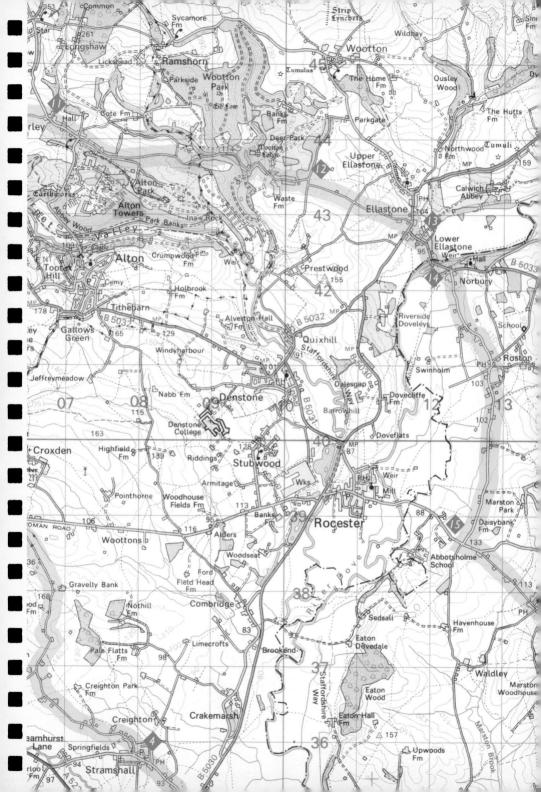

3 *Staffordshire Moorlands*

A ride through remote and enchanting countryside, with a diverse past, visiting several highlights as you explore the hills, ridges and valleys of the Staffordshire part of the National Park. The route twice crosses the county boundary into Derbyshire around Hartington and follows the west bank of the River Dane in Cheshire. The end of the ride winds through the impressive Roaches and their accompanying outcrops which form the foreground to the superb view from Morridge, across the Cheshire Plain, soon after leaving Leek.

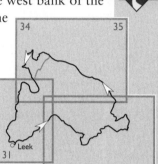

Start

Tourist Information Centre, Stockwell Street/Market Place, Leek

P Plenty in Leek

Distance and grade

49 km (30 miles)

Moderate

Terrain

Some long climbs from Leek to the Mermaid Inn and from Longnor to Axe Edge. Shorter climbs to Butterton and out of Wolfscote Dale. The route round Three Shire Heads is off-road and takes some effort (see on-road alternative from instruction 25)

Nearest railway

Stoke-on-Trent (6 km (10 miles) SW of Leek)

Refreshments

Plenty of choice in **Leek**
Mermaid Inn, **Morridge**
Shop and PH in **Butterton**
Manifold Valley Hotel, **Hulme End**
Plenty of choice in **Hartington** *and*
Longnor   *Flash Bar Shop on A53 at*
Quarnford

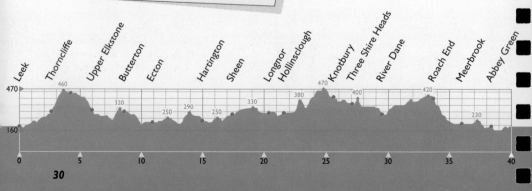

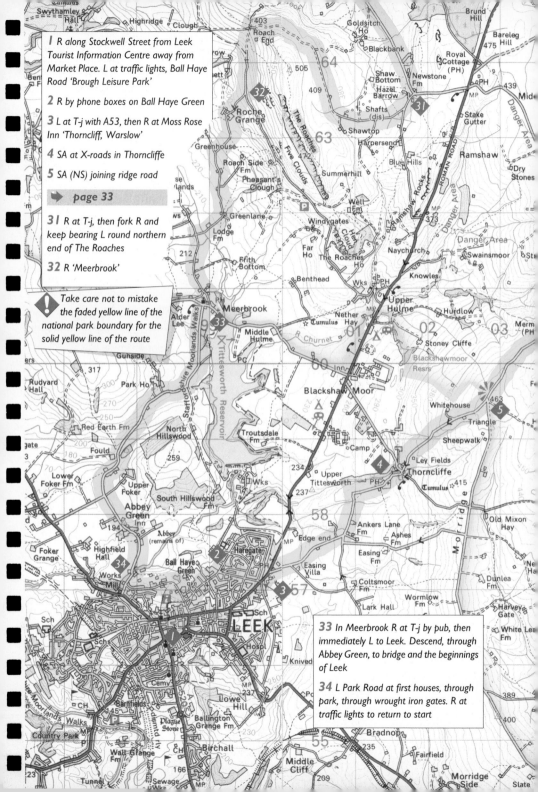

1 R along Stockwell Street from Leek Tourist Information Centre away from Market Place. L at traffic lights, Ball Haye Road 'Brough Leisure Park'

2 R by phone boxes on Ball Haye Green

3 L at T-j with A53, then R at Moss Rose Inn 'Thorncliff, Warslow'

4 SA at X-roads in Thorncliffe

5 SA (NS) joining ridge road

➡ page 33

31 R at T-j, then fork R and keep bearing L round northern end of The Roaches

32 R 'Meerbrook'

⚠ Take care not to mistake the faded yellow line of the national park boundary for the solid yellow line of the route

33 In Meerbrook R at T-j by pub, then immediately L to Leek. Descend, through Abbey Green, to bridge and the beginnings of Leek

34 L Park Road at first houses, through park, through wrought iron gates. R at traffic lights to return to start

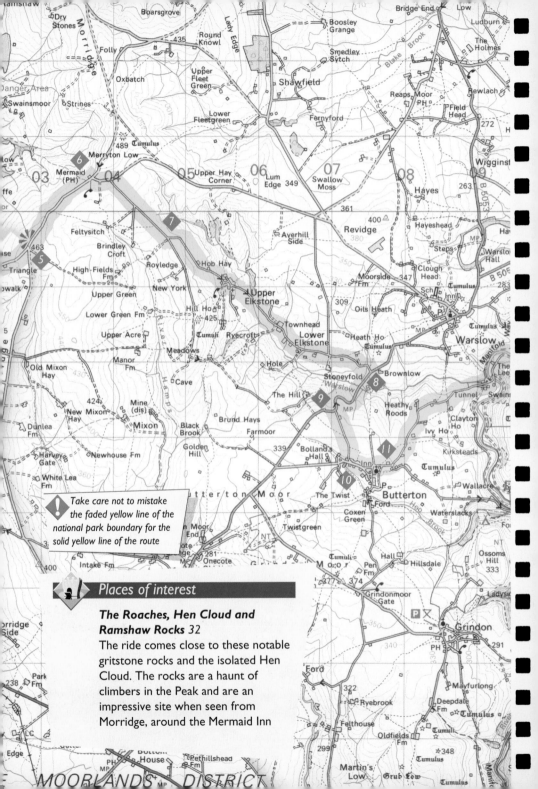

! Take care not to mistake the faded yellow line of the national park boundary for the solid yellow line of the route

Places of interest

The Roaches, Hen Cloud and Ramshaw Rocks *32*

The ride comes close to these notable gritstone rocks and the isolated Hen Cloud. The rocks are a haunt of climbers in the Peak and are an impressive site when seen from Morridge, around the Mermaid Inn

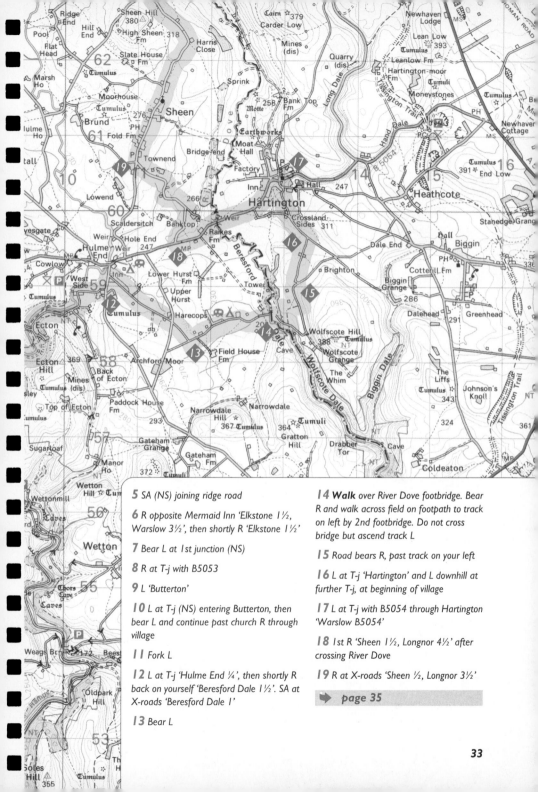

5 SA (NS) joining ridge road

6 R opposite Mermaid Inn 'Elkstone 1½, Warslow 3½', then shortly R 'Elkstone 1½'

7 Bear L at 1st junction (NS)

8 R at T-j with B5053

9 L 'Butterton'

10 L at T-j (NS) entering Butterton, then bear L and continue past church R through village

11 Fork L

12 L at T-j 'Hulme End ¼', then shortly R back on yourself 'Beresford Dale 1½'. SA at X-roads 'Beresford Dale 1'

13 Bear L

14 **Walk** over River Dove footbridge. Bear R and walk across field on footpath to track on left by 2nd footbridge. Do not cross bridge but ascend track L

15 Road bears R, past track on your left

16 L at T-j 'Hartington' and L downhill at further T-j, at beginning of village

17 L at T-j with B5054 through Hartington 'Warslow B5054'

18 1st R 'Sheen 1½, Longnor 4½' after crossing River Dove

19 R at X-roads 'Sheen ½, Longnor 3½'

➡ *page 35*

▲ *The Roaches from Hen Cloud*

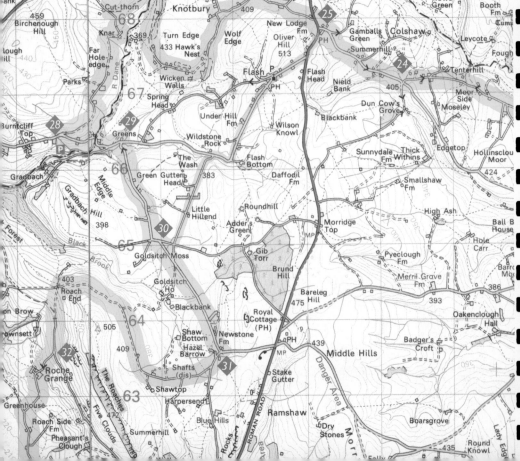

20 L at oblique T-j 'Longnor ¼, Leek 11'

21 R at X-roads in Longnor 'Buxton 6½ B5053, then 2nd L 'Hollinsclough 2, Flash 4½'

22 1st R 'Hollinsclough 1¼'

23 SA in Hollinsclough and up steep road 'Unsuitable for motors'

24 R at grass triangle T-j after 2 km (1½ miles)

25 R at T-j with A53, then immediately L 'Knotbury 1' (**Or** L onto A53 then 1st R through Flash, then L soon after sharp RH bend. SA at X-roads, then bear L)

26 Bear L, then sharp L at drive to Knotbury Lee Farm. Go down track in valley bottom; in about 800 m (½ mile) follow track as it bears R and contours round through almost 180° in about 1 km, to valley head with the track fence/wall on left. Bridleway joins obliquely on left

27 Cross bridge, below the confluence of two streams, at Three Shire Heads. L sharp back on yourself on bank of River Dane and follow rough track climbing the west side of the valley to tarmacked road. L back on yourself at T-j with metalled road, then descend steeply to sharp RH bend and contour for about 1 km

28 L back on yourself at T-j

29 R 'Royal Cottage 2¾, Leek 7¼'

30 Sharp bend L, then fork R

31 R at T-j, then fork R and keep bearing L round northern end of The Roaches

32 R 'Meerbrook'

! Take care not to mistake the faded yellow line of the national park boundary for the solid yellow line of the route

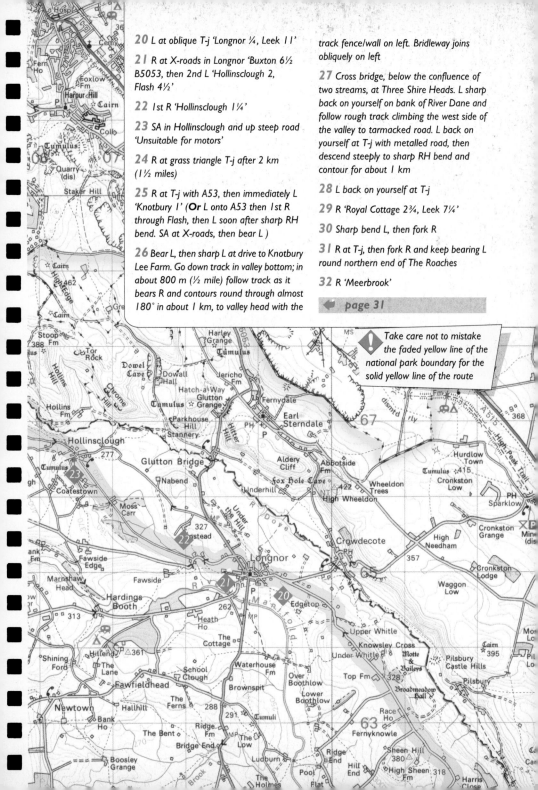

The Cloud and the Caldon Canal

A varied ride joining several different kinds of destination. The route passes Rudyard Reservoir and crosses The Cloud – an isolated hill with extensive views across the Cheshire Plain. The summit can be reached by foot either from the eastern flank of the hill, north of Cloud Side, or from Timbersbrook. To join the rural backwater of the Caldon Canal towpath, towards the end of the route, you will need a permit from British Waterways. Call their office at Marple on 0161 427 1079 for more details.

Start

Tourist Information Centre, Stockwell Street/Market Place, Leek

P Plenty of facilities in Leek

Distance and grade

40 km (25 miles)

Easy/moderate

Terrain

The sections by Rudyard Reservoir out to Rushton Spencer and back into Leek beside the canal are gentle. Some climbs around The Cloud and just before Biddulph Moor, but generally an easy ride

Nearest railway

Congleton (3 km (2 miles) from Timbersbrook) Stoke-on-Trent (6 km (10 miles) SW of Leek)

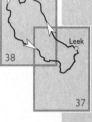

Leek

38

37

Refreshments

Plenty of choice in **Leek**
Pubs at **Rushton Spencer** and **Timbersbrook**
Plenty of choice in **Congleton** (3 km (2 miles) off the route at instruction 7)
Tea room at **Biddulph Grange** (for visitors)
Railway Centre cafe, **Cheddleton**

Leek   River Churnet   Rushton Spencer   Timbersbrook   Poolfold   Biddulph Moor   Longsdon

310
280
230   310   230
190   190
170
140   190

0   5   10   15   20   25   30   35   40

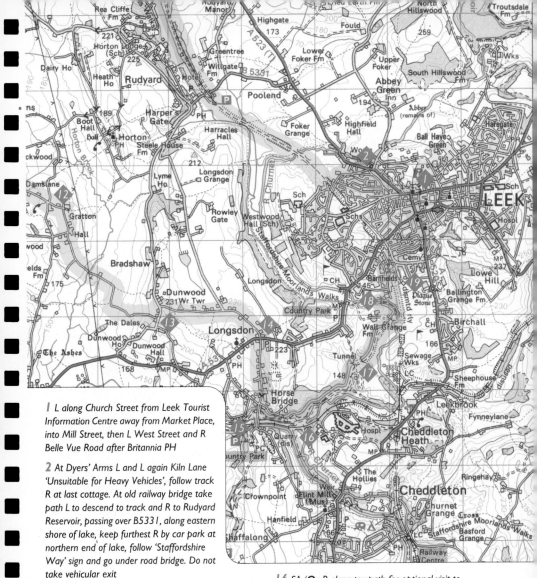

1 L along Church Street from Leek Tourist Information Centre away from Market Place, into Mill Street, then L West Street and R Belle Vue Road after Britannia PH

2 At Dyers' Arms L and L again Kiln Lane 'Unsuitable for Heavy Vehicles', follow track R at last cottage. At old railway bridge take path L to descend to track and R to Rudyard Reservoir, passing over B5331, along eastern shore of lake, keep furthest R by car park at northern end of lake, follow 'Staffordshire Way' sign and go under road bridge. Do not take vehicular exit

➡ **page 39**

12 SA at X-roads 'Leek 4¼', then bear R

13 L at T-j 'Rudyard 1¾, Leek 3, Rushton 5¼', then R 'Longsdon 1, Leek 3'

14 SA across X-roads with A53 in Longsdon 'Wall Grange ¾' and downhill along Sutherland Road to Caldon Canal

15 Through gap R at bridge and R onto canal towpath

16 SA (**Or** R along towpath for optional visit to Cheddleton)

17 Follow track up steps and over hill between hedges where canal goes through tunnel

18 At end of canal, cross bridge R, then follow path L into Barnfield Road (NS)

19 In about a 460 m (500 yd) take narrow lane R, cross bridge, then L at junction with road, R Selbourne Road, L at T-j with A520 (Compton Road) and R at parish church into Church Street to return to start

3 Leave track in about 1 km by Knot Inn where L, then fork R 'Woodhouse Lane 1¼'

4 2nd L 'Woodhouse Green ¼, Biddulph 5, Congleton 5'

5 R at T-j along road high up on eastern side of The Cloud 'Cloud Side ½'

6 L at X-roads 'Congleton'

7 L at X-roads in Timbersbrook

8 SA at X-roads, then L at T-j (not sharp L back on yourself) Overton Road

9 4th L by '30 mph' sign

10 In Biddulph Moor, SA at X-roads Chapel Lane, then L Cottage Lane and SA at X-roads Leek Lane 'Leek 7', bearing R in 1 km

11 L at X-roads 'Horton 1½, Leek 6', then fork R 'Gratton, Endon'

12 SA at X-roads 'Leek 4¼', then bear R

13 L at T-j 'Rudyard 1¾, Leek 3, Rushton 5¼', then R 'Longsdon 1, Leek 3'

Places of interest

Biddulph Grange *9 (just off the route)*
Biddulph Grange is a late 19th-century mansion which became a hospital and has recently had the gardens (which date back to 1845) magnificently restored by the National Trust. Not open Mondays or Tuesdays

Cheddleton *16 (just off the route)*
A notable industrial settlement which developed where James Brindley's Caldon Canal met the turnpike road. The flint mill supplied powder for the pottery trade and became a museum in the 1960s. There is a railway museum in the old station (in picturesque Tudor style) and there are plans to establish a steam railway

▼ Rudyard Reservoir

5 The Goyt Valley and Macclesfield Forest

A notable exploration of the millstone grit country between Macclesfield and Buxton, visiting the quiet villages of Pott Shrigley and Kettleshulme, and the wilder countryside of the Goyt Valley, Axe Edge and Macclesfield Forest. The first section of the route, along the Middlewood Way, has a good tarmac surface with several gateways to negotiate and one light-controlled road crossing.

Start
Macclesfield Town Hall

P Several public car parks in Macclesfield

Distance and grade
50 km (31 miles)

Moderate/ strenuous

Terrain
Few level sections, however, you ride down most of the sharpest hills. The main climbs are from Bollington to Brink Farm, from Kettleshulme to Old Nick, up the Goyt Valley and into Macclesfield Forest

Nearest railway
Macclesfield

▶ Axe Edge Moor

Refreshments
Plenty of choice in **Macclesfield**
Pubs in **Bollington**
Tea Cosy tea rooms and pubs in **Kettleshulme**
Shop in **Quarndon** and PH in **Flash**
Pubs in **Allgreave** and **Wildboarclough**

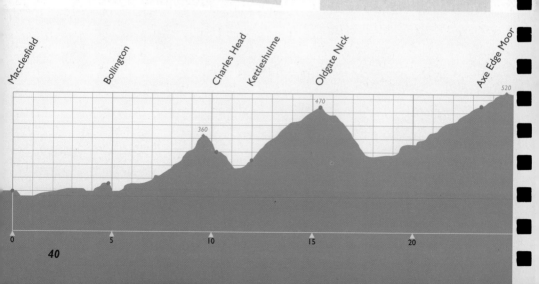

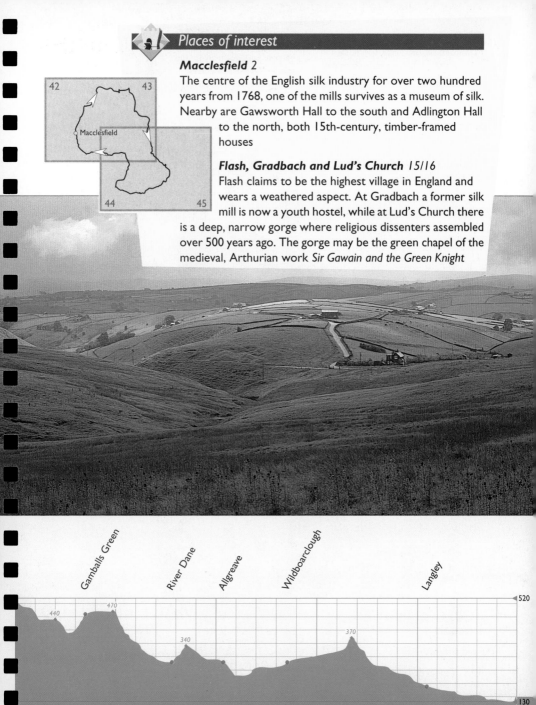

Places of interest

Macclesfield 2

The centre of the English silk industry for over two hundred years from 1768, one of the mills survives as a museum of silk. Nearby are Gawsworth Hall to the south and Adlington Hall to the north, both 15th-century, timber-framed houses

Flash, Gradbach and Lud's Church 15/16

Flash claims to be the highest village in England and wears a weathered aspect. At Gradbach a former silk mill is now a youth hostel, while at Lud's Church there is a deep, narrow gorge where religious dissenters assembled over 500 years ago. The gorge may be the green chapel of the medieval, Arthurian work *Sir Gawain and the Green Knight*

1 Facing outwards from the main entrance to Macclesfield Town Hall, turn R, then R again at traffic lights into Hibel Road and descend to roundabout. Take 2nd exit (in effect SA)

2 Pass entrance to supermarket, then L and go through gateway on left (adjoining exit from supermarket) to join Middlewood Way. After about 2 km (1¼ miles) the Middlewood Way crosses the A523 Silk Road dual carriageway

3 After a deviation L to go round a yard built across the old railway route (on foot) R at T-j with Grimshaw Lane and pass under aqueduct

4 L Chancery Lane where road bears R, then bear L North Street

5 R Shrigley Road 'Pott Shrigley, Whaley Bridge'

6 R Barkstonedale in Pott Shrigley 'Kettleshulme 3, Whaley Bridge 5'

7 L at T-j 'Kettleshulme, Whaley Bridge B5470'

8 R 'Goyt Valley 3'

9 L at T-j 'Buxton 5' and though gate in 2 km (1¼ miles) keeping reservoir on your left

10 R at T-j at head of Goyt Valley , then immediately L (NS)

11 SA at X-roads across A537 (NS), then L and immediately R to cross the A54 (NS) and over Axe Edge Moor

➡ page 45

19 L after 6 km (3¾ miles) 'Forest Chapel ¾' and SA at top of hill 'Langley 2½'

20 Bear R in Langley

21 Bear R in Sutton Lane Ends 'Macclesfield 2'

22 R at T-j with A523

23 R at traffic lights into Sutherland Road, continuing past railway station on R, bear R under railway line, then L at T-j, L again at roundabout and at traffic lights to enter Jordangate and return to start

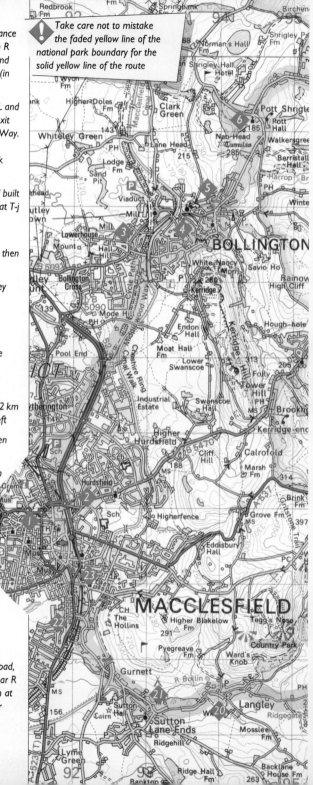

Take care not to mistake the faded yellow line of the national park boundary for the solid yellow line of the route

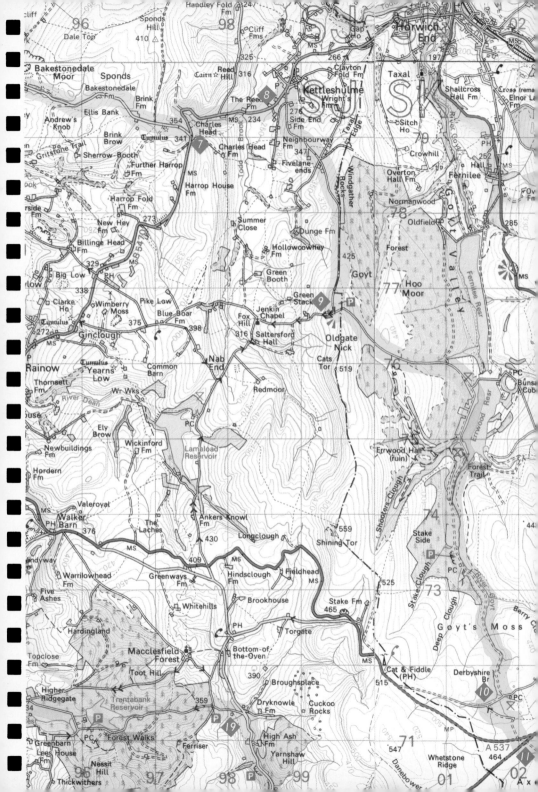

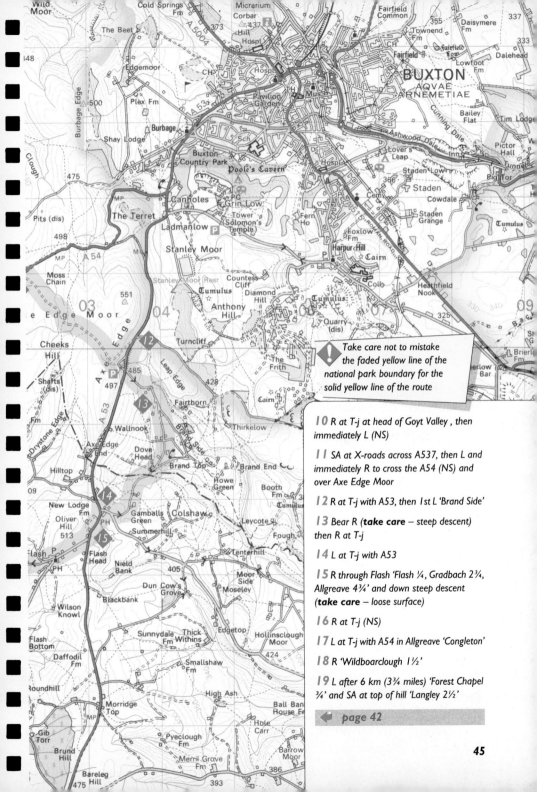

Take care not to mistake the faded yellow line of the national park boundary for the solid yellow line of the route

10 R at T-j at head of Goyt Valley , then immediately L (NS)

11 SA at X-roads across A537, then L and immediately R to cross the A54 (NS) and over Axe Edge Moor

12 R at T-j with A53, then 1st L 'Brand Side'

13 Bear R (**take care** – steep descent) then R at T-j

14 L at T-j with A53

15 R through Flash 'Flash ¼, Gradbach 2¾, Allgreave 4¾' and down steep descent (**take care** – loose surface)

16 R at T-j (NS)

17 L at T-j with A54 in Allgreave 'Congleton'

18 R 'Wildboarclough 1½'

19 L after 6 km (3¾ miles) 'Forest Chapel ¾' and SA at top of hill 'Langley 2½'

◀ page 42

Winnats and Tideswell

A ride of many contrasts, passing over the quieter millstone grit between New Mills and Mam Tor and again west of Dove Holes. The route crosses limestone country around the popular destinations of Castleton and Tideswell. There is a notable descent at Winnats Pass – a spectacular gorge and a favourite of mountain bikers.

Start

New Mills Central Station

P Several sites in New Mills

Distance and grade

55 km (34 miles)
Moderate/ strenuous

Terrain

A mixture of the hilly and the more level upland plateau. Steep climbs from Wash, Bradwell, Tideswell and Monk's Dale while Rushup Edge is easier. The descent into Combs is sharply bended and needs care. The off-road alternative at instruction 12 is slower and more demanding than the on-road equivalents

Refreshments

Plenty of choice in **New Mills**
Squirrels Inn, **Chinley**
Tea room at the Chestnut Centre
Plenty of choice in **Castleton,**
Bradwell *and* **Tideswell**
Midland Hotel, **Peak Dale**
Beehive Hotel, **Combs**

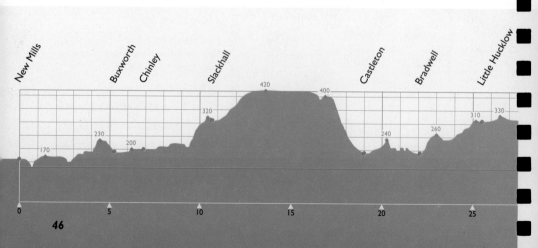

New Mills Central
Chinley, Hope and
Doves Holes

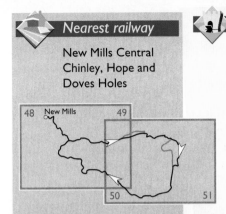

New Mills 1

A mill town, once a centre of the calico printing trade. The former railway line between the town and Hayfield has been made into the Sett Valley Trail for walkers, cyclists and horse riders

Bradwell 13

A homely, former lead-mining village at the foot of Bradwell Dale. Bagshawe's Cavern, at the far end of an old lead mine and down 100 steps or so, is about 800 m (½ mile) long.

▲ Winnats Pass

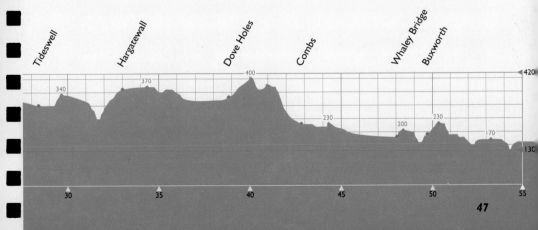

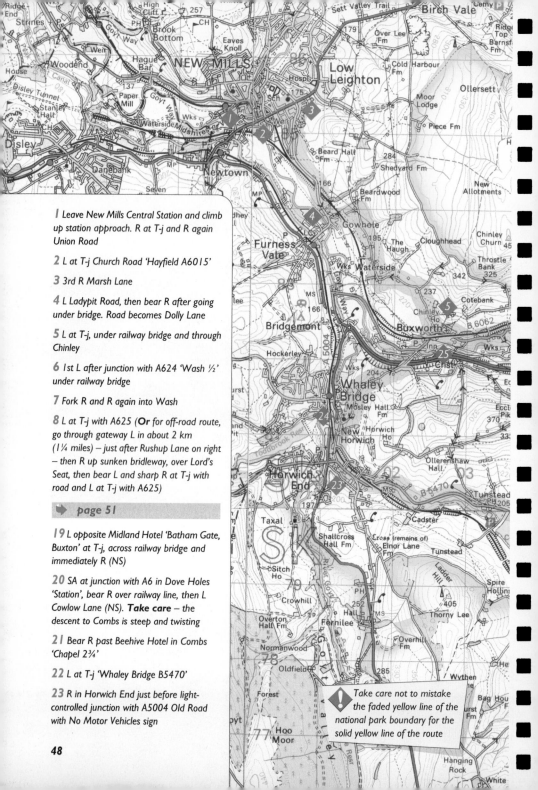

1 Leave New Mills Central Station and climb up station approach. R at T-j and R again Union Road

2 L at T-j Church Road 'Hayfield A6015'

3 3rd R Marsh Lane

4 L Ladypit Road, then bear R after going under bridge. Road becomes Dolly Lane

5 L at T-j, under railway bridge and through Chinley

6 1st L after junction with A624 'Wash ½' under railway bridge

7 Fork R and R again into Wash

8 L at T-j with A625 (**Or** for off-road route, go through gateway L in about 2 km (1¼ miles) – just after Rushup Lane on right – then R up sunken bridleway, over Lord's Seat, then bear L and sharp R at T-j with road and L at T-j with A625)

➡ **page 51**

19 L opposite Midland Hotel 'Batham Gate, Buxton' at T-j, across railway bridge and immediately R (NS)

20 SA at junction with A6 in Dove Holes 'Station', bear R over railway line, then L Cowlow Lane (NS). **Take care** – the descent to Combs is steep and twisting

21 Bear R past Beehive Hotel in Combs 'Chapel 2¾'

22 L at T-j 'Whaley Bridge B5470'

23 R in Horwich End just before light-controlled junction with A5004 Old Road with No Motor Vehicles sign

! Take care not to mistake the faded yellow line of the national park boundary for the solid yellow line of the route

48

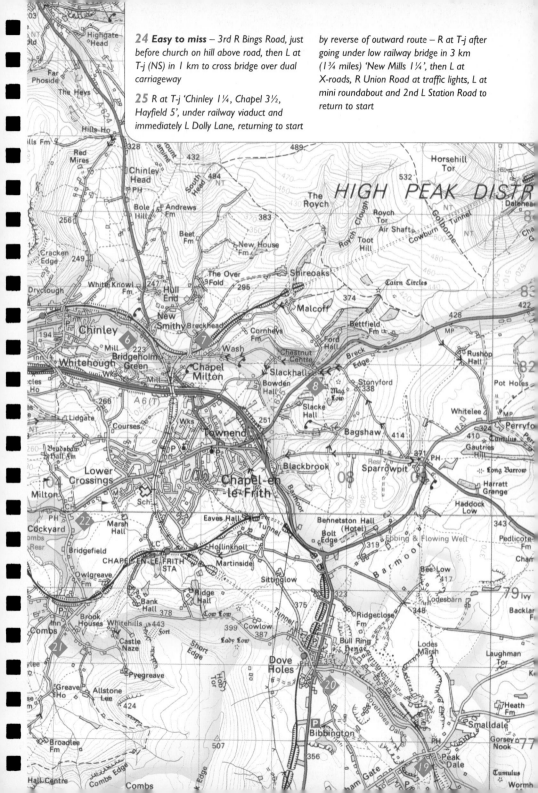

24 Easy to miss – 3rd R Bings Road, just before church on hill above road, then L at T-j (NS) in 1 km to cross bridge over dual carriageway

25 R at T-j 'Chinley 1¼, Chapel 3½, Hayfield 5', under railway viaduct and immediately L Dolly Lane, returning to start

by reverse of outward route – R at T-j after going under low railway bridge in 3 km (1¾ miles) 'New Mills 1¼', then L at X-roads, R Union Road at traffic lights, L at mini roundabout and 2nd L Station Road to return to start

HIGH PEAK DISTRICT

Take care not to mistake the faded yellow line of the national park boundary for the solid yellow line of the route

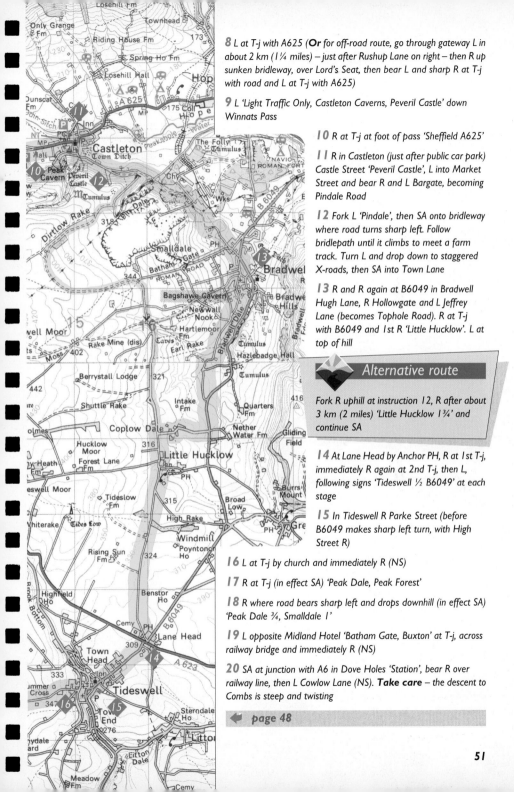

8 L at T-j with A625 (**Or** for off-road route, go through gateway L in about 2 km (1¼ miles) – just after Rushup Lane on right – then R up sunken bridleway, over Lord's Seat, then bear L and sharp R at T-j with road and L at T-j with A625)

9 L 'Light Traffic Only, Castleton Caverns, Peveril Castle' down Winnats Pass

10 R at T-j at foot of pass 'Sheffield A625'

11 R in Castleton (just after public car park) Castle Street 'Peveril Castle', L into Market Street and bear R and L Bargate, becoming Pindale Road

12 Fork L 'Pindale', then SA onto bridleway where road turns sharp left. Follow bridlepath until it climbs to meet a farm track. Turn L and drop down to staggered X-roads, then SA into Town Lane

13 R and R again at B6049 in Bradwell Hugh Lane, R Hollowgate and L Jeffrey Lane (becomes Tophole Road). R at T-j with B6049 and 1st R 'Little Hucklow'. L at top of hill

Alternative route

Fork R uphill at instruction 12, R after about 3 km (2 miles) 'Little Hucklow 1¾' and continue SA

14 At Lane Head by Anchor PH, R at 1st T-j, immediately R again at 2nd T-j, then L, following signs 'Tideswell ½ B6049' at each stage

15 In Tideswell R Parke Street (before B6049 makes sharp left turn, with High Street R)

16 L at T-j by church and immediately R (NS)

17 R at T-j (in effect SA) 'Peak Dale, Peak Forest'

18 R where road bears sharp left and drops downhill (in effect SA) 'Peak Dale ¾, Smalldale 1'

19 L opposite Midland Hotel 'Batham Gate, Buxton' at T-j, across railway bridge and immediately R (NS)

20 SA at junction with A6 in Dove Holes 'Station', bear R over railway line, then L Cowlow Lane (NS). **Take care** – the descent to Combs is steep and twisting

◀ page 48

7 *Last of the Summer Wine*

A tour of the magnificent countryside between Barnsley and Holmfirth. Though it only touches on the National Park, and passes through parts of the lowland West Riding, it is mostly in the Pennine millstone grit country. An alternative part of the Trans-Pennine Cycle Route is due to run along the former railway line between Dunford Bridge and Penistone and will give an easier return to Penistone when it is opened.

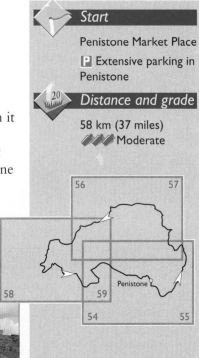

Start

Penistone Market Place

🅿 Extensive parking in Penistone

Distance and grade

58 km (37 miles)

Moderate

◀ The Holme Valley

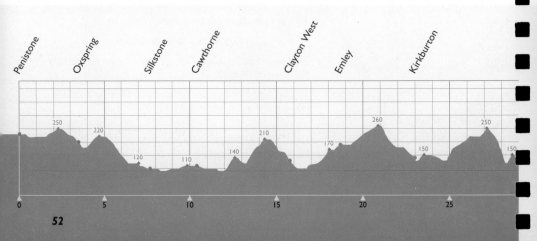

Terrain

The countryside is almost entirely upland Several steep-walled valleys to be crossed and long sections along hilltops. Some off-road cycling round the head of the Holme Valley

Nearest railway

Penistone and Stockwood

Places of interest

Cawthorne 10

A village with a late 19th-century church and a delightful local museum. To its west lies Cannon Hall Country Park and Museum. The house and grounds date from the 18th century. There is also a regimental museum which includes a model display of the Charge of the Light Brigade, Victorian kitchens (open in the summer) and a Visitor Centre with exhibits relating to the house, gardens and village

Holmfirth 24

Now, fittingly, the home of BBC TV's *Last of the Summer Wine*, it was the home of the comic picture postcard in the late 19th century and the company's proprietor, James Bamforth, tried to establish an English film industry here in the early years of this century. There is a postcard museum

Refreshments

Plenty of choice in **Penistone**
Spencer Arms, **Cawthorne**
Cafes at Cannon Hall Country Park (Sundays) and Garden Centre (opposite main car park)
Pubs in **Emley** and **Kirkburton**
Plenty of choice in **Holmfirth**
Pubs in **Upperthong**
Pubs in **Dunford Bridge** and **Victoria**

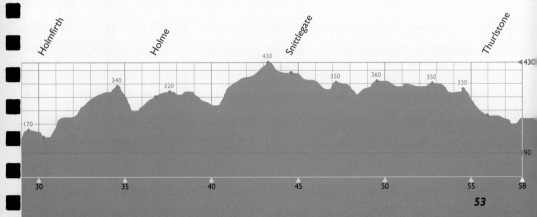

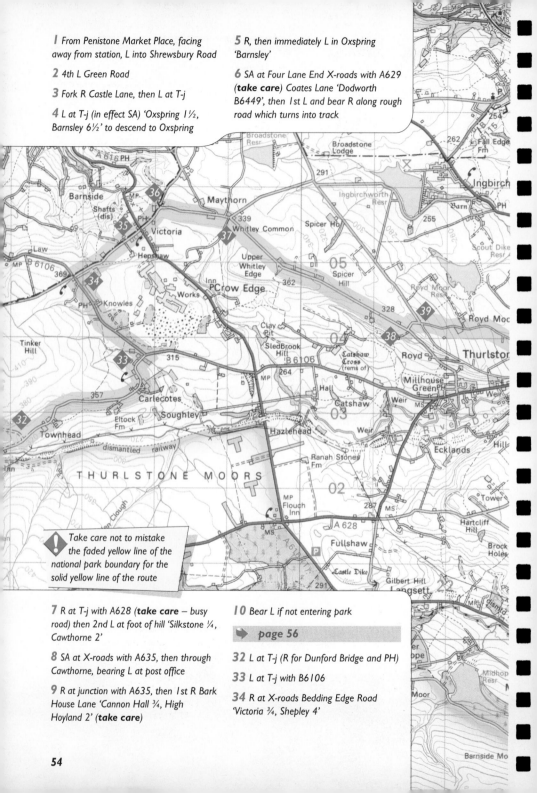

1 *From Penistone Market Place, facing away from station, L into Shrewsbury Road*

2 *4th L Green Road*

3 *Fork R Castle Lane, then L at T-j*

4 *L at T-j (in effect SA) 'Oxspring 1½, Barnsley 6½' to descend to Oxspring*

5 *R, then immediately L in Oxspring 'Barnsley'*

6 *SA at Four Lane End X-roads with A629 (**take care**) Coates Lane 'Dodworth B6449', then 1st L and bear R along rough road which turns into track*

Take care not to mistake the faded yellow line of the national park boundary for the solid yellow line of the route

7 *R at T-j with A628 (**take care** – busy road) then 2nd L at foot of hill 'Silkstone ¼, Cawthorne 2'*

8 *SA at X-roads with A635, then through Cawthorne, bearing L at post office*

9 *R at junction with A635, then 1st R Bark House Lane 'Cannon Hall ¾, High Hoyland 2' (**take care**)*

10 *Bear L if not entering park*

➥ **page 56**

32 *L at T-j (R for Dunford Bridge and PH)*

33 *L at T-j with B6106*

34 *R at X-roads Bedding Edge Road 'Victoria ¾, Shepley 4'*

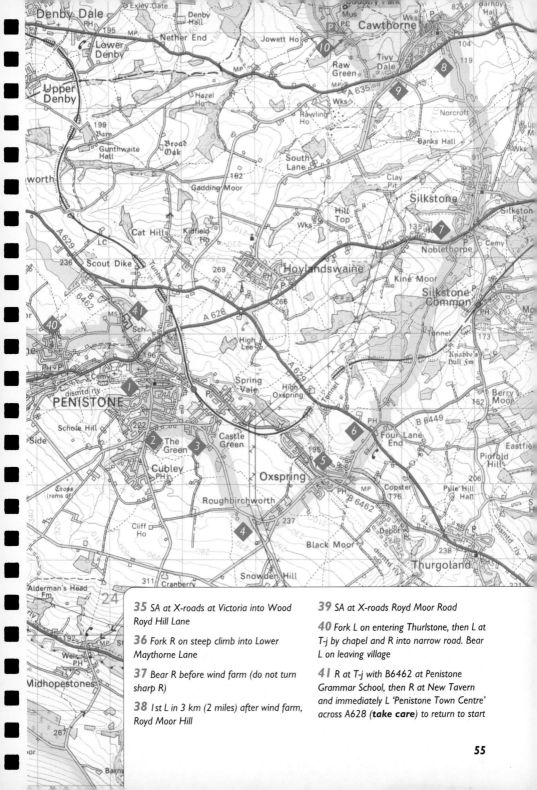

35 SA at X-roads at Victoria into Wood Royd Hill Lane

36 Fork R on steep climb into Lower Maythorne Lane

37 Bear R before wind farm (do not turn sharp R)

38 1st L in 3 km (2 miles) after wind farm, Royd Moor Hill

39 SA at X-roads Royd Moor Road

40 Fork L on entering Thurlstone, then L at T-j by chapel and R into narrow road. Bear L on leaving village

41 R at T-j with B6462 at Penistone Grammar School, then R at New Tavern and immediately L 'Penistone Town Centre' across A628 (**take care**) to return to start

9 R at junction with A635, then 1st R Bark House Lane 'Cannon Hall ¾, High Hoyland 2' (**take care**)

10 Bear L if not entering park

11 Sharp L back on yourself on entering High Hoyland 'Clayton West 1¼'

12 R at T-j with A636 at far end of Clayton West (**take care** – fast cars) then 3rd L in 365 m (400 yd) Kiln Lane 'Emley 1½'

13 L at T-j approaching Emley 'Emley ½'

14 Fork R at base of TV mast 'Jagger Lane'

15 Road bears L

16 R B6116 and immediately L in Kirkburton

17 Cross A629 (**take care**) at oblique X-roads 'Stocksmoor 1, Thurstonland 2, New Mill 3'

18 R Stocksmoor Road 'Stocksmoor' by PH

19 Road bears L

20 SA across A616 Luke Lane, then bear L

21 R at T-j

22 4th L onto bridleway Berry Back Lane and take lower track at fork

23 Very obliquely R onto A635 (**take care**)

➡ **page 58**

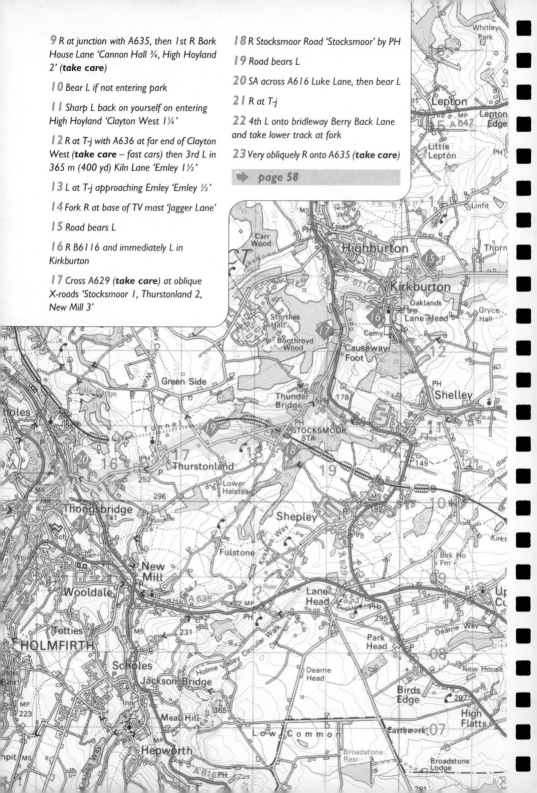

18 R Stocksmoor Road 'Stocksmoor' by PH

19 Road bears L

20 SA across A616 Luke Lane, then bear L

21 R at T-j

22 4th L onto bridleway Berry Back Lane and take lower track at fork

23 Very obliquely R onto A635 (**take care**)

24 In centre of Holmfirth bear R at junction with B6106 Victoria Street, then L at T-j with A6024 and fork 1st R Upperthong Lane

25 L by PH Broad Lane and L again Dean Road

26 L at T-j by Ford Inn 'Holmfirth, Greenfield', then SA at X-roads Green Gate Lane

27 R at T-j with A6024 in Holme

28 L onto sandy forest track, contour round, then across Yateholme Dam and rise

29 Where track bears L at house, take track R 'public bridleway' onto Kirklees Way and follow uphill

30 Hard R at 5-way junction of minor routes at end of track

31 R towards Dunford Bridge by 'Welcome to Barnsley' sign

32 L at T-j (R for Dunford Bridge and PH)

33 L at T-j with B6106

34 R at X-roads Bedding Edge Road 'Victoria ¾, Shepley 4'

35 SA at X-roads at Victoria into Wood Royd Hill Lane

36 Fork R on steep climb into Lower Maythorne Lane

37 Bear R before wind farm (do not turn sharp R)

 ← **page 55**

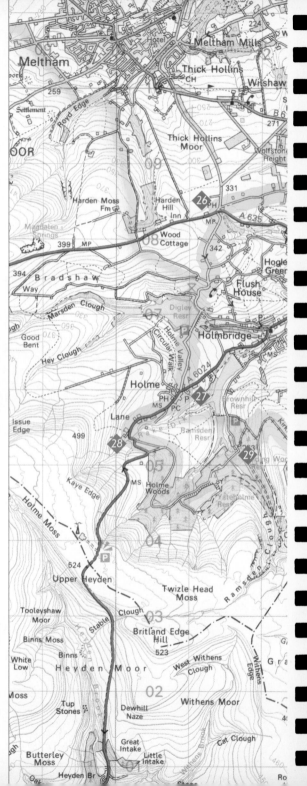

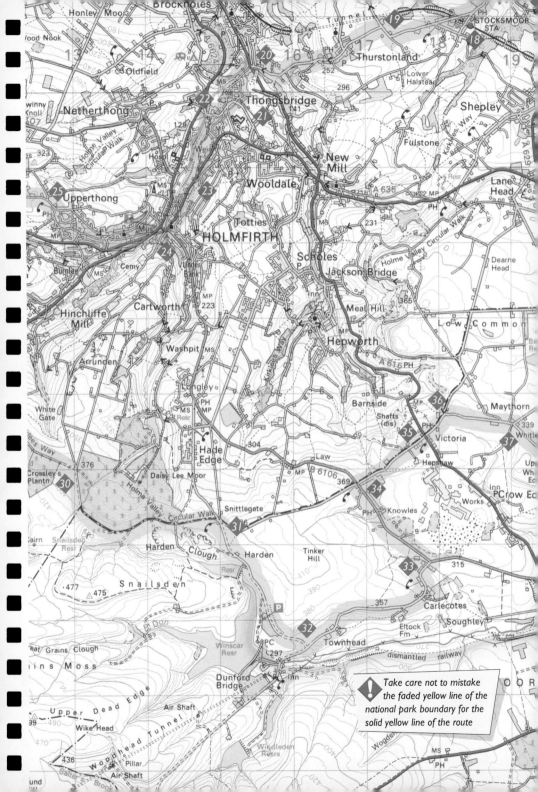

Take care not to mistake the faded yellow line of the national park boundary for the solid yellow line of the route

8 Loxley Valley

A ride around the moors and reservoirs west of the built-up area but almost entirely within the boundaries of the metropolitan district of Sheffield. Through the villages of High and Low Bradfield and the hamlet of Strines. High-level sections offer good views across the River Don to Wharncliffe and along the Loxley Valley. This route can be linked with Route 19, for the stronger cyclist, joining at Low Bradfield.

Start

Junction of Myers Grove Lane with Wood Lane at the Malinbridge end

P There are several public off-street car parks in the city, but none close to the start of the ride. People using nearby pubs may be able to use their car parks – please ask

▶ *Bradfield Dale from High Bradfield*

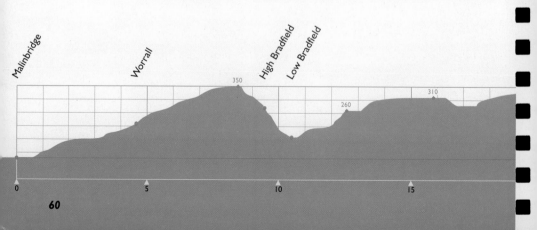

Distance and grade

38 km (24 miles)
 Moderate/
strenuous

Terrain

Several climbs up the
steep sides of Loxley
Valley, but there are
long upland sections
between Worrall and
High Bradfield and
from Strines to Ughill.
The return to
Malinbridge follows an
old track

Nearest railway

Sheffield

Places of interest

Strines *8/9*
The Inn was once a small manor house.
Across the valley is Boot's Folly, built for a
Sheffield contractor who lived nearby to
keep his workforce occupied

Loxley Valley *15*
A valley of reservoirs, formerly a centre of
the metal industry when the river powered
numerous small workshops. The dam
above Bradfield (Dale Dyke) broke in 1865
resulting in the deaths of some 240 people
and the destruction of about 600 buildings
downstream

Refreshments

Old Horns Inn, **High Bradfield**
Strines Inn, **Strines**
PH in **Dungworth** *(SA instead
of L at instruction 13)*
Pubs in and around **Malinbridge**

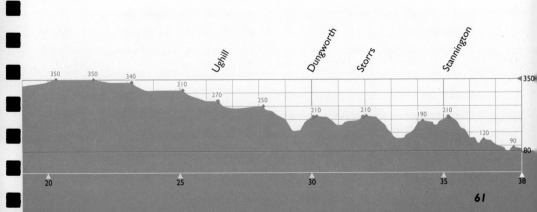

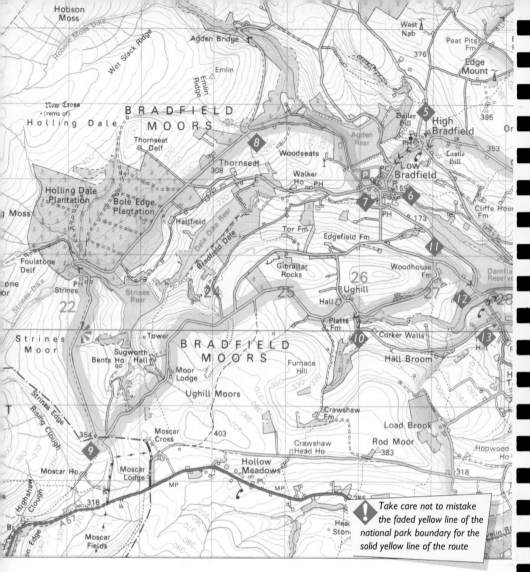

Take care not to mistake the faded yellow line of the national park boundary for the solid yellow line of the route

1 L from the eastern end of Myers Grove Lane and L into Stannington Road

2 Bear L into Loxley Road, just after crossing river, fork R into Wisewood Lane (becoming Hallowmoor Road) and SA at X-roads into Rural Lane

3 Obliquely L at T-j (NS)

4 L Kirk Edge Road at triangular junction entering Worrall 'High Bradfield 3, Loxley 1¼'

5 Bear L Little Lane 'Loxley 3, Sheffield 7', then R at T-j and L Woodfall Lane 'Low Bradfield ½, Dungworth 2½'.

Take care – steep gradients and risk of missing junctions

6 L The Sands at 1st T-j in Low Bradfield, then sharp R Smithy Bridge Road 'Dungworth 1½, Sheffield 7', across River Loxley and R at 2nd T-j Fairhouse Lane 'Penistone 10, Strines'

7 1st R Windy Bank 'Midhopestones 7, Penistone 10'

8 L at T-j (NS)

9 L just after cattle grid about 2 km (1¼ miles) after passing through Strines hamlet 'Ughill 3, Dunghill 5'

10 4th L in about 5 km (3½ miles) Ughill Wood Lane 'Bradfield 2'

11 R at T-j 'Dungworth 1¼'

12 R at T-j (in effect SA) 'Dungworth ¾, Sheffield 6', then R uphill 'Dungworth ½, Stannington 2½'

13 1st L Dungworth Green 'Storrs 1', passing school R

14 Bear L in Storrs 'Loxley 1¼'. **Take care** descending steep, twisting lane

15 R 'Stannington ½, Sheffield 5'

16 L Acorn Way (NS) and bear L at bus turning place into Acorn Drive

17 L at T-j (Greaves Lane sign further down road) going SA past 'Public Byway' sign downhill. The surface deteriorates once the last house is passed on the right. In about 460 m (500 yd) come to Robin Hood PH on left, and join its access drive, then L at T-j into Myers Grove Lane to return to start

9 Burbage, Eyam and Froggatt

This ride mixes the shade of Ecclesall Woods, the high moorland southwest of Sheffield, the edges on the east of the Derwent Valley. Linking the little town of Hathersage, the Barrell Road through Bretton and the villages of Great Hucklow, Foolow and Eyam which were once busy with mining and quarrying. It can be started at several points *en route* but for convenience the instructions start at Dore Station.

Start

Dore Station

P There is some on-road parking in Abbeydale Road, Dore, beside Ecclesall Woods Public parking at Ringinglow and at Upper Burbage bridge

Distance and grade

50 km (31 miles)
Moderate

Refreshments

Cafe at **Abbeydale** Industrial Hamlet
Norfolk Arms PH, **Ringinglow**
Plenty of choice in **Hathersage** and **Eyam**
Barrell Inn, **Bretton**
Queen Anne PH, **Great Hucklow**
Lazy Landlord PH, **Foolow**
Several pubs between **Froggatt** and **Bradway**

▶ Rilley Graves at Eyam

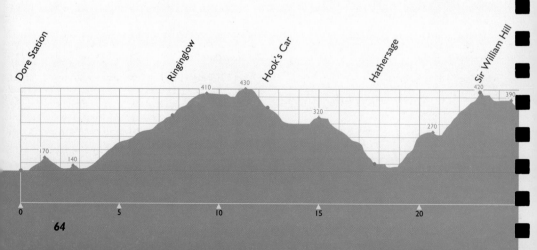

Three main climbs: from Dore up to Burbage Rocks, from Leadmill Bridge to Sir William Hill and out of the Derwent Valley over Froggatt Edge. They mostly call for stamina rather than great effort, though there are some sharp pitches on the climb from Hathersage to Sir William Hill

Nearest railway

Sheffield, Dore, Hathersage and Grindleford

Places of interest

Hathersage 10

Hathersage was an industrial town until this century, with various metalwork trades linked with wire-drawing: nailmaking, pinmaking and needles. The leading family was once that of Eyre. Charlotte Bronte used the name, and other local elements in 'Jane Eyre', where the town is called 'Morton', and her 'Thornfield Hall' may be modelled on North Lees Hall

Eyam 17

Once a mining and still a quarrying centre. Eyam's chief historical association is with the outbreak of Plague which, it is supposed, arrived in a bolt of cloth from London in 1665. William Mompesson, the Rector, with his predecessor Thomas Stanley (who had been ejected under the Act of Conformity in 1662) organised a quarantine of the villagers, over 80% of whom died. There is a museum facing the car park in the former Methodist church at the west end of the village

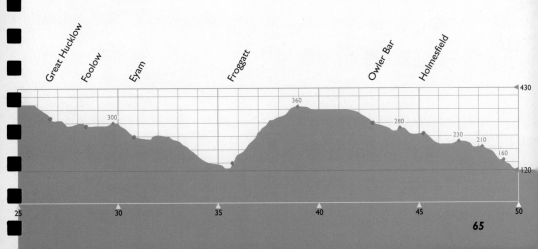

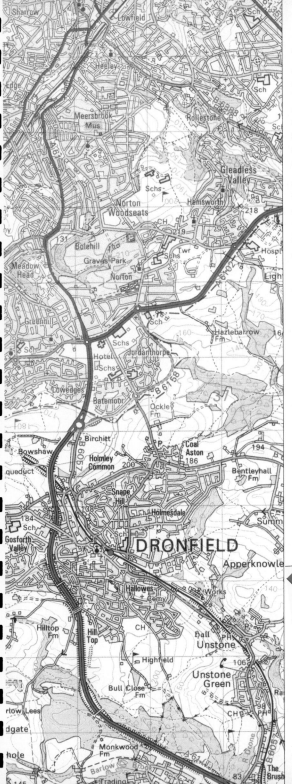

1 R at the exit from Dore Station into Abbeydale Road

2 L into Ecclesall Wood 'Public Bridleway' (opposite Beauchief Gardens). From sign 'Public Bridleway to Dore' take next track R and continue SA, bearing gently R and climbing. After about 800 m (½ mile) track turns further R ('Horse Riding Prohibited' on left) and begin to drop down, passing between two 'Public Footpath' signs

3 Track leads to Abbey Lane where R and then L onto further bridleway, just before Abbey Croft cul-de-sac. **Take care** – busy road. Fork L in woods where a signed public footpath crosses the route

4 R onto Whirlowdale Road which crosses track

5 L Whirlowdale Crescent and ascend to T-j along Millhouses Lane, where L, then bear R into Silverdale Road at upper end

6 SA at X-roads into Knowle Lane and SA (becomes Ringinglow Road)

➡ **page 68**

21 At Owler Bar (one-way – **take care**) pass Peacock Inn and take turning 'Holmesfield, Dronfield B6054' by Moorlands Inn. SA through Holmesfield, Dronfield Woodhouse and Mickley, following signs for B6054

22 R at T-j in Upper Bradway 'Sheffield (A61)', then L 'Dore 2, Millhouses 2¼' and down Twentywell Lane to T-j with A621 where R 'Sheffield A621' and immediately R again to return to Dore Station

! Take care not to mistake the faded yellow line of the national park boundary for the solid yellow line of the route

7 Fork R 'Ladybower 6' after Burbage Rocks car park and just before cattle grid

8 R 'Ladybower 5'

9 R 'Ladybower 4'

10 L into Jagger's Lane, then L at T-j and R onto B6001 'Grindleford 3, Baslow 5' in Hathersage

11 R at brow of hill just after Plough PH

12 R at T-j (NS)

13 R (in effect SA) onto track over Sir William Hill where sealed road bears sharp L. R (in effect SA) at end of track, following Barrell Road along ridge (**Or** sharp L for short cut to Eyam, then L again at T-j just after Eyam Museum on right to join main route at instruction 17)

14 L at entrance to Great Hucklow 'Grindlow ¼'. SA through Grindlow

15 L at T-j (NS)

16 SA in Foolow, following signs for 'Eyam' or 'Eyam, Grindleford'

17 L at T-j entering Square in Eyam 'Hathersage B6521'

18 **Take care** – R at T-j with B6001 'Bakewell B6001'. L 'Froggatt' and descend steeply to bridge across River Derwent, then L Hallowgate and R uphill at Rose Cottage

19 L at T-j 'Calver B6054 1½' and up across face of Froggatt Edge through woods

20 R at T-j 'Dronfield B6054, Owler Bar 2'

◀ page 67

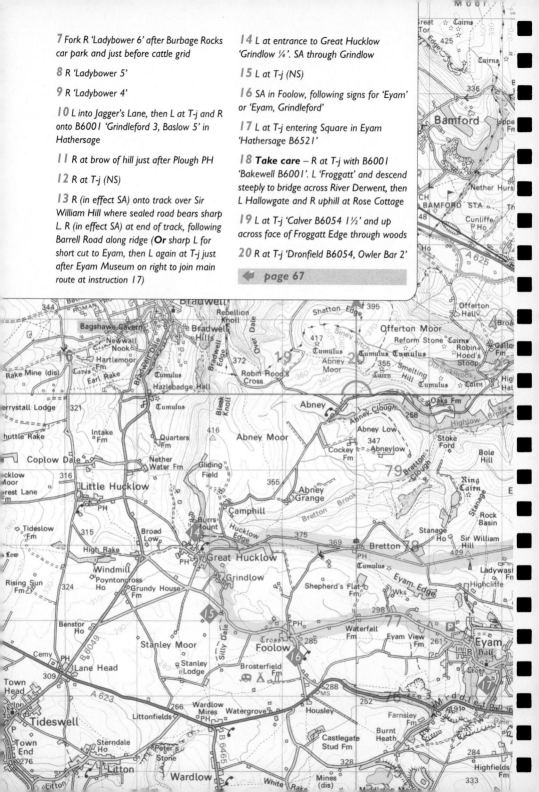

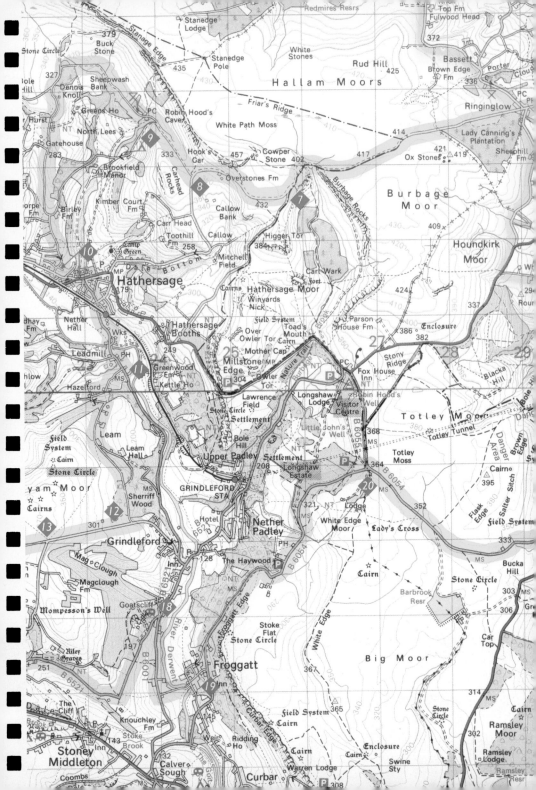

10 ◆ *Between Chesterfield and Bakewell*

A ride with much to offer. There are several off-road sections on a variety of surfaces between Calver and Hell Bank and excellent views on the climb from Common Side to Bole Hill, over High Rake and as you leave Bakewell. Between Longstone and Bakewell the ride follows the Monsal Trail. This is a section of the old Midland Railway's main line between London and Manchester which closed down in the 1960s and has been converted into a route for non-motor traffic.

Start

Chesterfield Tourist Information Centre

P Several long-stay car parks in Chesterfield

Distance and grade

48 km (30 miles)

🏔🏔🏔🏔 Moderate/ strenuous

Terrain

A route set mostly against the lie of the land with lengthy climbs from Common Side and from Beeley Lodge and sharp ascents from Calver (off-road) and Bakewell. The descents into the Derwent Valley (over Curbar Edge and into Edensor) need some care

Refreshments

Plenty of choice in **Chesterfield**
Tea shop in **Barlow**
Tea shop and PH at **Calver Bridge**
Eyre Arms, **Hassop**
The Crispin PH, **Great Longstone**
Plenty of choice in **Bakewell**
Tea shop in **Edensor**
Cafe at Calton Lees garden centre
Devonshire Arms, **Beeley**

Chesterfield — Upper Newbold — Barlow — Common Side — Rumbling Street — Baslow Edge — Curbar — Longstone Edge

290 300 270 380 140

0   5   10   15   20

Places of interest

Chesterfield 1

The core of the town is the mostly traffic-free Market Place, which deserves some time to visit. The crooked spire of the parish church catches the eye, but the rest of the church is of interest. Much dates from the 14th and 15th centuries and there are side chapels which reflect the medieval wealth of the town

Edensor 17

A village on the Chatsworth estate (pronounced 'Enser') planned by Joseph Paxton (the Duke's head gardener) and aided in the design of the houses by John Robertson of Derby. The village displays a range of Victorian villa architecture. Buildings date from 1839 to around 1850 and were probably an attempt to create an 'improved' model village some time after the old settlement had been removed

◀ Edensor

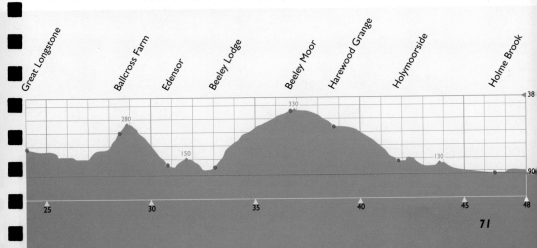

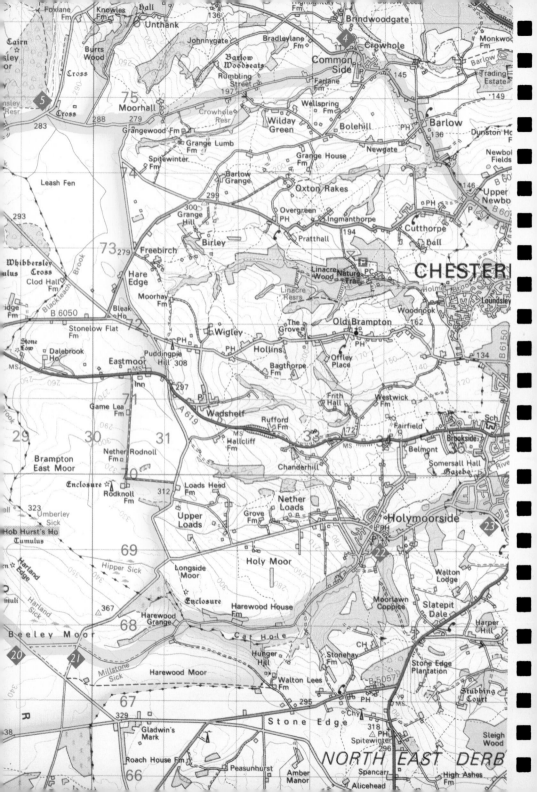

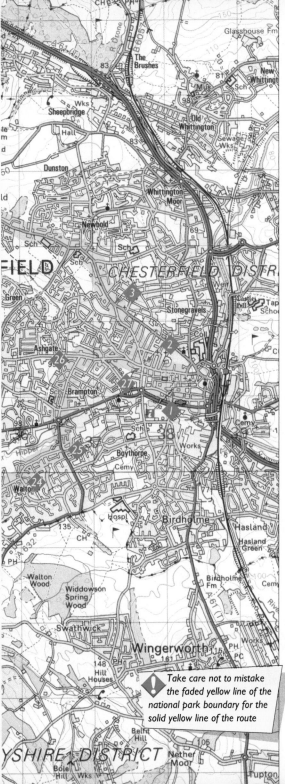

1 From Chesterfield Tourist Information Centre cross Market Place with Market Hall on your right, then up Soresby Street and SA at X-roads with Rose Hill. L at T-j with Saltersgate

2 R where Saltersgate becomes Ashgate Road, into Compton Street, bear L into West Street, then along Hawksley Avenue

3 L at T-j with main road (B6051, NS). SA for about 6 km (4 miles) through Upper Newbold, Barlow and Common Side

4 L at triangular junction just before delimitation sign at end of Common Side and uphill for 3 km (2 miles) Farley Lane (NS). SA to enter Peak National Park near top of climb

5 L at T-j 'Baslow 4'

➡ page 74

20 L after 800 m (½ mile) on Beeley Moor where open triangular green begins (NS)

21 SA at X-roads after 548 m (600 yd) (NS)

22 R at X-roads by Bull's Head PH in Holymoorside

23 L in 2 km (1¼ mile) Park Hall Avenue, L again at T-j Somersby Avenue (becomes Breckland Road)

24 L at T-j Moorland View Road and bear R

25 L at further T-j after 800 m (½ mile) and descend to mini-roundabout where SA, then SA again at X-roads with traffic lights and at further X-roads in 90 m (100 yd) into Old Hall Road

26 R at T-j

27 SA at X-road with traffic lights and R into one-way street Clarence Road and downhill to T-j with traffic lights where L, then bear L into West Bars and dismount at 'No Entry' signs. The Tourist Information Centre is on your right a further 90m (100 yd) along Low Pavement

⚠ Take care not to mistake the faded yellow line of the national park boundary for the solid yellow line of the route

6 L at T-j with A621 'Baslow 1½', then R at staggered X-roads 'Curbar 2'. R after car park and descend Curbar Edge. **Take care** – steep descent

7 R at T-j opposite Bridge Inn and R at T-j onto A623 'Stockport, Manchester A623'

8 1st L 'Calver village' bearing L where Main Street becomes High Street

9 L at T-j with B6001 'Bakewell', then shortly after T-j go through field gate on your right and follow track across hillside

10 Bear R where track comes in obliquely on your left

11 Bear R onto unsealed road along ridge of Longstone Edge. **Take care** – quarry traffic. Pass over High Rake and descend to cattle grid

12 Through metal gate and L onto road, then bear R down Longstone Edge, bearing L near foot

13 L at T-j entering Great Longstone 'Rowland, Hassop, Ashford' (in effect SA) through village and bear R

14 Sharp L in 400 m (¼ mile) just before bridge over road, then immediately R at end of fence onto access path to 'Monsal Trail', turning away from bridge along Trail towards Bakewell (information notice by path entrance). Continue along Monsal Trail for about 3 km (2 miles)

15 At Bakewell Station take path on R alongside side of station buildings nearest to you into car park. Turn L at car park exit and L again 'Unsuitable for Lorries' over bridge across former railway line. Pass golf course and after about 800 m (½ mile) road turns R back on itself steeply uphill

16 After about 2 km (1¼ miles) take rough track forking R by sycamore tree. **Take care** – poor surface. After a further 2 km (1¼ miles) road surface becomes sealed and enters Edensor village

17 Keep village green on your R cross cattle grid. R onto B6012 and after 2 km (1¼ miles) cross bridge

18 Bear L where sign shows No through road, and climb along clearly defined track once tarmac ends

19 L at junction with surfaced road

⚠ Take care not to mistake the faded yellow line of the national park boundary for the solid yellow line of the route

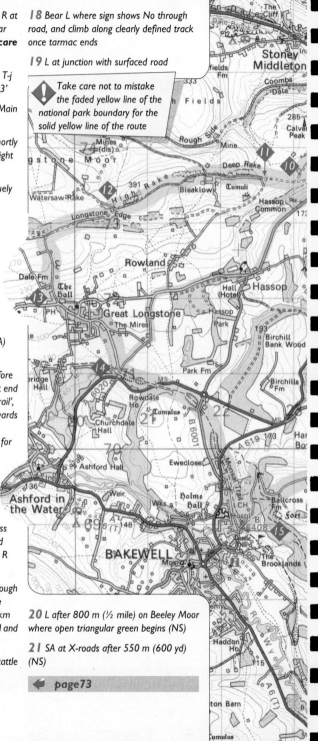

20 L after 800 m (½ mile) on Beeley Moor where open triangular green begins (NS)

21 SA at X-roads after 550 m (600 yd) (NS)

◀ page 73

Alternative route

From Calver to instruction 14 After L turn onto B6001 at end of Calver village, SA to Hassop where R 'Towland, Great Longstone'. Take 2nd L Longreave Lane and shortly before T-j with overbridge L onto access path 'Monsal Trail' joining route at instruction 14

Alternative route

Via Beeley From Beeley Lodge (instruction 18) bear R on B6012. 2nd L just after bus shelter 'Beeley village' and R 'Beeley Moor', keeping Devonshire Arms on your left. After 2 km (1½ miles) bear R where track joins from left and continue from instruction 20

From Cromford, visiting industrial sites and quiet countryside

A short ride with plenty of interest and plenty of contrast. There is much industrial archaeology in the early part of the ride but it then becomes very much more rural. The waterside at Ogston Reservoir or the picturesque village of Ashover offer excellent spots for a picnic.

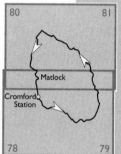

Start

Cromford Station

P Leawood Pumping Station. Matlock Station

Distance and grade

34 km (21 miles)
🥾🥾🥾 Moderate

Terrain

The start and finish are hilly but the middle section from Crich to the head of the Amber Valley is easy until Ashover is reached. A steady ascent to the head of the valley is followed by an exhilarating drop back to the Derwent Valley

Nearest railway

Matlock
Cromford

▶ *Cromford*

Refreshments

Plenty of pubs on the route from **Cromford** *to* **Kelstedge**
National Tramway Museum tea rooms, **Crich**
Plenty of choice in **Matlock** *and* **Matlock Bath**

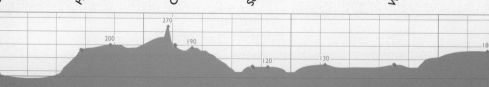

South Wingfield 4

The romantic ruins of medieval Wingfield Manor are notable. One of Mary Queen of Scots' many places of incarceration in or near the Peak, it was damaged during the English Civil War and much of its masonry re-used in the 18th century. The village church, off-route down Church Lane, is mainly 13th century.

Matlock 19–21

A collection of villages which grew as a 19th-century spa, once the road through Scarthin Nick (now the A6) was opened in 1818, and the railway from Ambergate in 1849. Tourism is now chiefly at Matlock Bath, with the diversions of attractions such as Gulliver's World, the Heights of Abraham, attainable by a funicular, and the Peak District Mining Museum

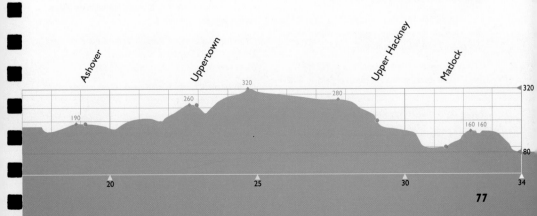

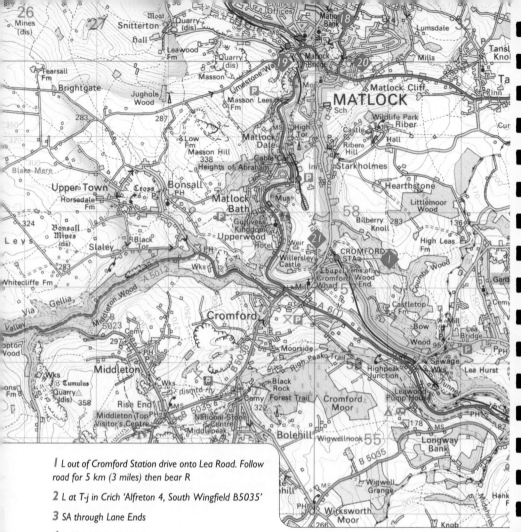

1 L out of Cromford Station drive onto Lea Road. Follow road for 5 km (3 miles) then bear R

2 L at T-j in Crich 'Alfreton 4, South Wingfield B5035'

3 SA through Lane Ends

4 In South Wingfield L Inns Lane 'Moorwood Moor, Tansley' and then immediately R High Road. Fork L in about 180 m (200 yd) Wessington Lane

5 L 'Matlock 5¾ A615' at T-j with A615, then R Cross Lane 'Higham' on entering Wessington where main road bears L – **take care**. R at T-j (NS)

6 Easy to miss – L after about 135 m (150 yd) 'Brackenfield' bearing sharp R 'Brackenfield' in 800 m (½ mile)

7 R at T-j by church 'Woolley Moor 1¾'

8 R at T-j 'Clay Cross, Tibshelf B6014', then 1st L just after crossing small arm of reservoir 'Woolley Moor'. Bear L in village

➡️ *page 81*

18 In Matlock Bank R at X-roads Bank Street. **Take care** – very steep in parts

19 In Matlock Bridge L at roundabout Causeway Road (becomes Causeway Lane, then Matlock Green) 'Motorway M1, A615 Chesterfield (A632)'

20 In Matlock Green R at X-roads Church Street (becomes Starkholmes Road, then Willersley Road/ Lane) 'Starkholmes'

21 L almost back on yourself at T-j Lea Road 'Lea, Holloway, Crich' and L again up Cromford Station approach

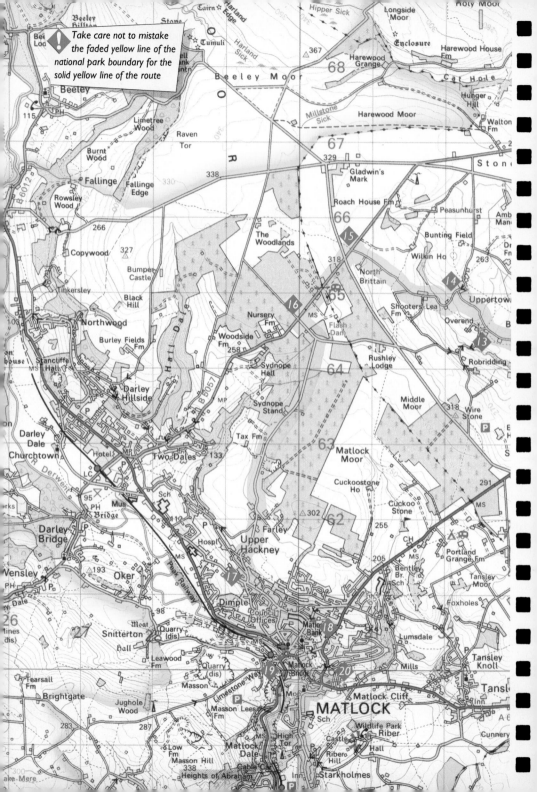

Take care not to mistake the faded yellow line of the national park boundary for the solid yellow line of the route

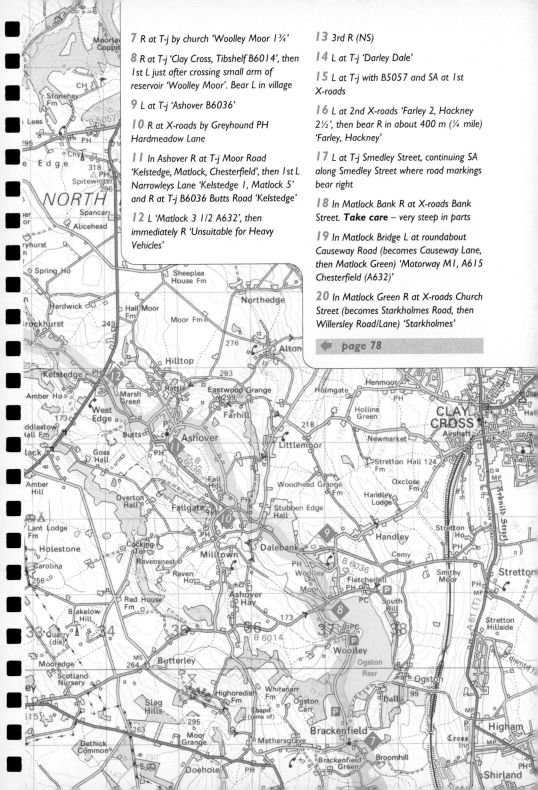

7 R at T-j by church 'Woolley Moor 1¾'

8 R at T-j 'Clay Cross, Tibshelf B6014', then 1st L just after crossing small arm of reservoir 'Woolley Moor'. Bear L in village

9 L at T-j 'Ashover B6036'

10 R at X-roads by Greyhound PH Hardmeadow Lane

11 In Ashover R at T-j Moor Road 'Kelstedge, Matlock, Chesterfield', then 1st L Narrowleys Lane 'Kelstedge 1, Matlock 5' and R at T-j B6036 Butts Road 'Kelstedge'

12 L 'Matlock 3 1/2 A632', then immediately R 'Unsuitable for Heavy Vehicles'

13 3rd R (NS)

14 L at T-j 'Darley Dale'

15 L at T-j with B5057 and SA at 1st X-roads

16 L at 2nd X-roads 'Farley 2, Hackney 2½', then bear R in about 400 m (¼ mile) 'Farley, Hackney'

17 L at T-j Smedley Street, continuing SA along Smedley Street where road markings bear right

18 In Matlock Bank R at X-roads Bank Street. **Take care** – very steep in parts

19 In Matlock Bridge L at roundabout Causeway Road (becomes Causeway Lane, then Matlock Green) 'Motorway M1, A615 Chesterfield (A632)'

20 In Matlock Green R at X-roads Church Street (becomes Starkholmes Road, then Willersley Road/Lane) 'Starkholmes'

← **page 78**

Two Trails and the Barmote

A ride along two of the old railway lines converted into trails for walkers, riders and cyclists. The trails can be busy on fine summer weekends and Bank holidays.

▲ *The High Peak Trail near Minninglow Hill*

Refreshments

Drinks and snacks at **Cromford Wharf, Middleton Top** and **Parsley Hay**
Teas at **Gotham Grange** and **Tissington**
Pubs in **Brassington**
Plenty of choice in **Wirksworth**

Start

Cromford Station or Wirksworth or the cycle hire centres at Middleton Top and Parsley Hay

P Cromford Station and Middleton Top Visitor Centre

Distance and grade

60 km (37 miles)
Easy

Terrain

The High Peak and Tissinton Trails offer easy cycling though there are two steep inclines near the Cromford start. There are climbs from the turning for Bradbourne and past Brassington on the return leg

Nearest railway

Cromford

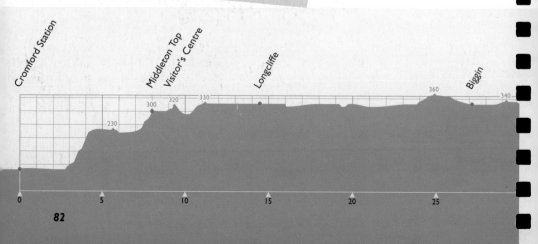

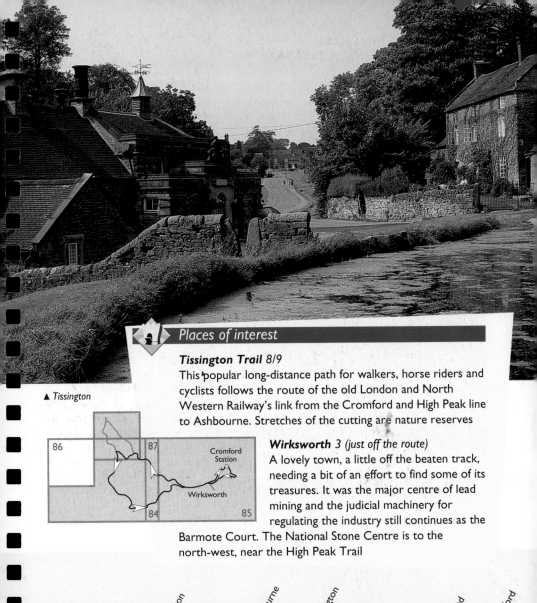

▲ Tissington

Places of interest

Tissington Trail 8/9

This popular long-distance path for walkers, horse riders and cyclists follows the route of the old London and North Western Railway's link from the Cromford and High Peak line to Ashbourne. Stretches of the cutting are nature reserves

Wirksworth 3 (just off the route)

A lovely town, a little off the beaten track, needing a bit of an effort to find some of its treasures. It was the major centre of lead mining and the judicial machinery for regulating the industry still continues as the Barmote Court. The National Stone Centre is to the north-west, near the High Peak Trail

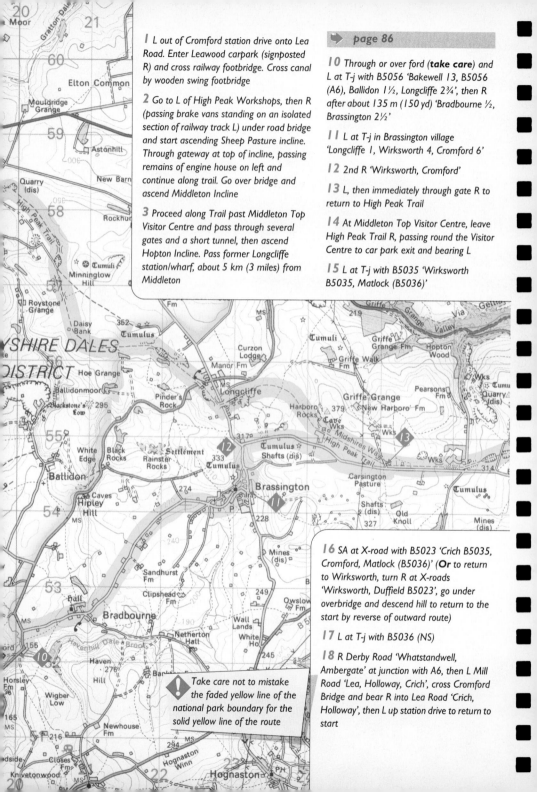

1 L out of Cromford station drive onto Lea Road. Enter Leawood carpark (signposted R) and cross railway footbridge. Cross canal by wooden swing footbridge

2 Go to L of High Peak Workshops, then R (passing brake vans standing on an isolated section of railway track L) under road bridge and start ascending Sheep Pasture incline. Through gateway at top of incline, passing remains of engine house on left and continue along trail. Go over bridge and ascend Middleton Incline

3 Proceed along Trail past Middleton Top Visitor Centre and pass through several gates and a short tunnel, then ascend Hopton Incline. Pass former Longcliffe station/wharf, about 5 km (3 miles) from Middleton

➡ **page 86**

10 Through or over ford (**take care**) and L at T-j with B5056 'Bakewell 13, B5056 (A6), Ballidon 1½, Longcliffe 2¾', then R after about 135 m (150 yd) 'Bradbourne ½, Brassington 2½'

11 L at T-j in Brassington village 'Longcliffe 1, Wirksworth 4, Cromford 6'

12 2nd R 'Wirksworth, Cromford'

13 L, then immediately through gate R to return to High Peak Trail

14 At Middleton Top Visitor Centre, leave High Peak Trail R, passing round the Visitor Centre to car park exit and bearing L

15 L at T-j with B5035 'Wirksworth B5035, Matlock (B5036)'

16 SA at X-road with B5023 'Crich B5035, Cromford, Matlock (B5036)' (**Or** to return to Wirksworth, turn R at X-roads 'Wirksworth, Duffield B5023', go under overbridge and descend hill to return to the start by reverse of outward route)

17 L at T-j with B5036 (NS)

18 R Derby Road 'Whatstandwell, Ambergate' at junction with A6, then L Mill Road 'Lea, Holloway, Crich', cross Cromford Bridge and bear R into Lea Road 'Crich, Holloway', then L up station drive to return to start

! Take care not to mistake the faded yellow line of the national park boundary for the solid yellow line of the route

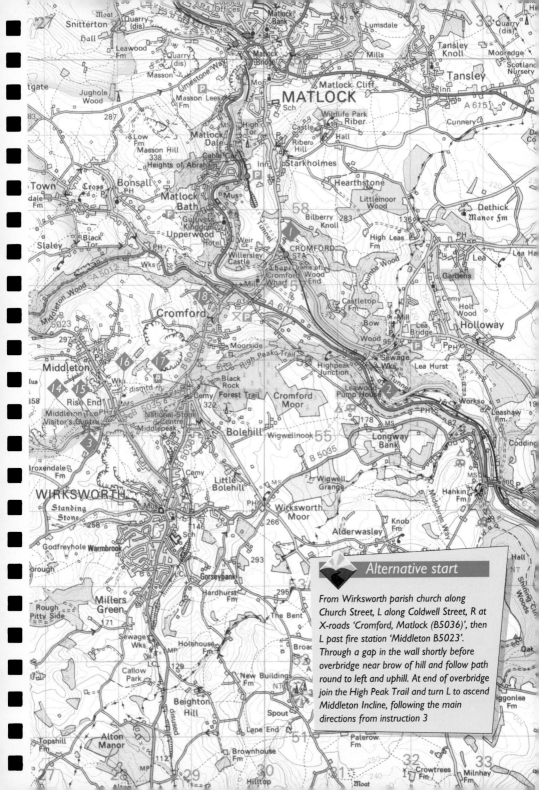

Alternative start

From Wirksworth parish church along Church Street, L along Coldwell Street, R at X-roads 'Cromford, Matlock (B5036)', then L past fire station 'Middleton B5023'. Through a gap in the wall shortly before overbridge near brow of hill and follow path round to left and uphill. At end of overbridge join the High Peak Trail and turn L to ascend Middleton Incline, following the main directions from instruction 3

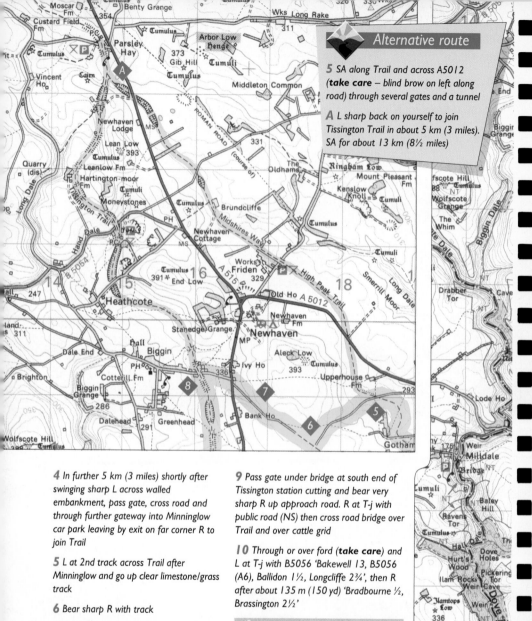

Alternative route

5 SA along Trail and across A5012 (**take care** – blind brow on left along road) through several gates and a tunnel

A L sharp back on yourself to join Tissington Trail in about 5 km (3 miles). SA for about 13 km (8½ miles)

4 In further 5 km (3 miles) shortly after swinging sharp L across walled embankment, pass gate, cross road and through further gateway into Minninglow car park leaving by exit on far corner R to join Trail

5 L at 2nd track across Trail after Minninglow and go up clear limestone/grass track

6 Bear sharp R with track

7 R at T-j 'Buxton A515, Newhaven 1', then immediately L Biggin Lane

8 R through wicket gate just before bridge, ascend to Trail, sharp L back on yourself and over bridge, continuing along Trail past Alsop en le Dale in about 5 km (3 miles)

9 Pass gate under bridge at south end of Tissington station cutting and bear very sharp R up approach road. R at T-j with public road (NS) then cross road bridge over Trail and over cattle grid

10 Through or over ford (**take care**) and L at T-j with B5056 'Bakewell 13, B5056 (A6), Ballidon 1½, Longcliffe 2¾', then R after about 135 m (150 yd) 'Bradbourne ½, Brassington 2½'

◀ page 84

Take care not to mistake the faded yellow line of the national park boundary for the solid yellow line of the route

13 Ilam, Hartington and Parwich

A ride with much to offer, no single outstanding feature, but several contrasting landscapes. The route runs across the plateau between the Dove and Manifold valleys, exploring the moorland to the west, the open countryside between Longnor and Hartington, and finally going off-road to Kniveton and returning to Ashbourne.

 Start

Tourist Information Centre, Market Square, Ashbourne

P Extensive long-term parking in Ashbourne and the cycle hire centre there

 Distance and grade

54 km (34 miles)

Moderate

 Terrain

This is a ride that is rarely level, but does not require anything like as much effort as

 Refreshments

Plenty of choice in **Ashbourne**
Tea room at **Ilam Hall**
Watts-Russell Arms, **Hopedale**
PH, cafe at craft centre in **Wetton**
Cavalier PH, **Grindon**
Shop and PH in **Butterton**
Old Butchers Arms, **Reaps Moor**
Plenty of choice in **Hartington**
Shop and PH in **Parwich**

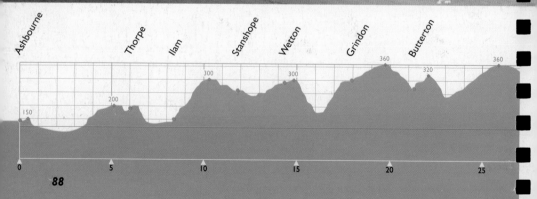

might be imagined.
Climbs from Ilam and
out of the Manifold
Valley are quite steep –
there is a lengthy rise
from Elkstone and a
short off-road rise after
Tissington

Nearest railway

Uttoxeter, 19 km
(12 miles) from start
Derby, 22 km
(14 miles) from start
Buxton, 14 km
(9 miles) from
instruction 21

*Background picture:
Musden Low, Ilam*

Places of interest

Hartington 27
A Cavendish manor which is now a
favourite place for day visitors. The 13th-
century St Giles' church has similarities to
Wirksworth's. The market was chartered
in 1203 and the large Market Place retains
the village mere. There is a rustic classical
market hall of 1811, and the youth hostel
(up the road towards Biggin) is an
attractive, early Jacobean stone building.
The village is now one of the places where
Stilton cheese is made

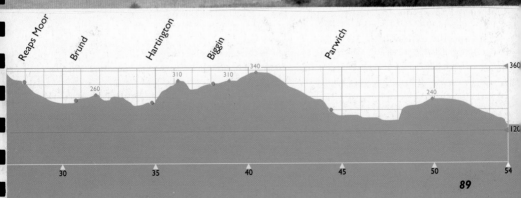

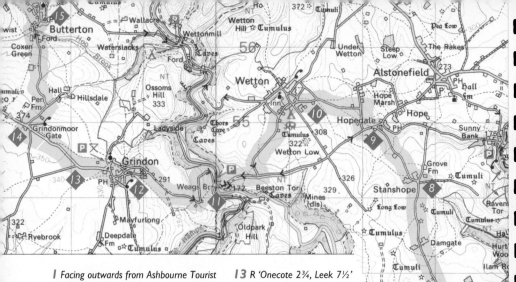

1 Facing outwards from Ashbourne Tourist Information Centre, R across Market Place towards Buxton Road where L and immediately L again into Union Street. R into Dove House Green

2 2nd L (in effect SA) Mappleton Lane

3 SA in Mappleton 'Thorpe 2¼, Dovedale'

4 L at T-j (NS)

5 *Easy to miss* 1st L into narrow lane between stone gateposts

6 L at T-j and immediately bear R 'Dovedale, Ilam 1½' **NB** cattle grid without warning sign on steep descent

7 R at T-j in Ilam village 'Alstonefield 3½, Wetton 4'

8 Bear L at Stanshope

9 L at T-j 'Wetton 1, Manifold Valley 1½', then immediately bear sharp R, then L to enter Wetton

10 R 'Wetton Mill 1¼, Manifold Valley, Butterton 2½' then L 'Grindon 2½, Manifold Valley' and bear L 'Single Track Road with Passing Places' in Wetton. R at T-j (**Take care** – very steep descent)

11 SA across bridge and X-roads with Manifold Track at Weags Bridge, then climb out of valley (**Take care** at junction)

12 Bear L at entry to Grindon, R at Cavalier PH, then L at triangular junction

13 R 'Onecote 2¾, Leek 7½'

14 R at T-j (in effect SA) 'Onecote 2¼, Warslow 3¾, Leek 7', then shortly R 'Butterton 1'

15 Go through ford on entering Butterton (**take care**) keep bearing L as you rise, then L at T-j 'Onecote 2¼, Warslow 2½'

➡ **page 93**

33 Enter Parwich and bear R down from Parwich Hall, then L with village shop facing you, pass village green and church on your left and SA 'Ballidon 1¾, Ashbourne 6¾'

34 Bear R on leaving Parwich

35 R at T-j 'Ballidon 1, Ashbourne 6'

36 R at T-j 'Ashbourne 5½ B5056 (A515); Fenny Bentley 3¼'

37 After 1 km, almost opposite turning to right 'Ford', L through gate and climb up track. Through further gate into open field at top of hill and bear R through gate near farm buildings (**not** gate SA). Through several more gates to T-j with road in Knivetonwood where R

38 R at T-j 'Ashbourne B5035'

39 After 2 km (1¼ miles) fork R

40 L at X-roads at end of Mill Road and descend Buxton Road to Market Place (2nd R) to return to start

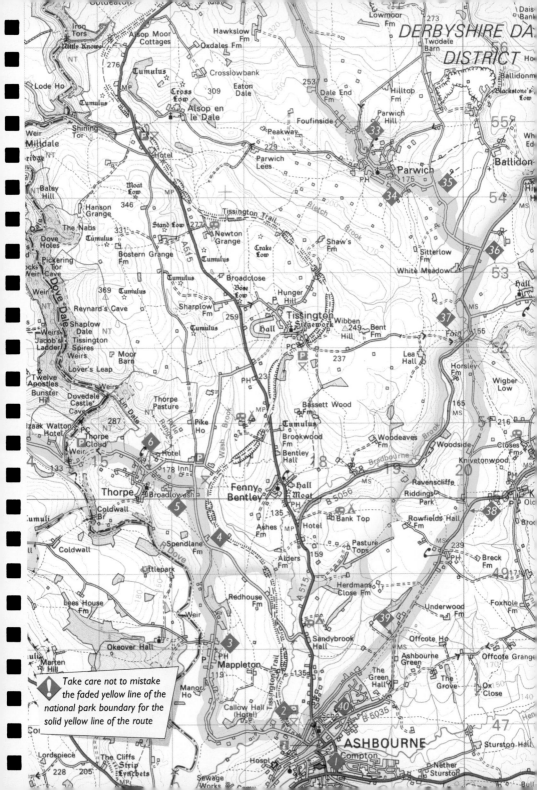

Take care not to mistake the faded yellow line of the national park boundary for the solid yellow line of the route

15 Go through ford on entering Butterton (**take care**) keep bearing L as you rise, then L at T-j 'Onecote 2¼, Warslow 2½'

16 R just past Butterton Post Office on left

17 R at T-j 'Warslow 1½, Longnor 5½ B5053'

18 L at foot of hill after about 800 m (½ mile) (NS)

19 1st R (NS)

20 SA at X-roads after 2 km (1¼ miles) 'Reapsmoor 1, Longnor 3½

21 R after 2 km (1½ miles) opposite church

22 SA at X-roads with B5053 'Brund 1¼'

23 **Easy to miss** – 2nd L after 1 km

24 1st R just after passing Brund Mill on left 'Sheen 1¼'

25 SA at offset X-roads 'Hartington 2', then bear R

26 L at T-j 'Hartington 1 B5054', cross R Dove in 800 m (½ mile) and enter Hartington in further 1 km

27 R past newsagents' before church 'Youth Hostel 250 yd'

28 3rd R on unsurfaced track about 230 m (250 yd) after YH on L. After about 1 km continue SA as other tracks join first from left then right and begin descent (**take care** – uneven surface)

29 R at T-j with metalled road (in effect SA) then 1st L Main Street 'Biggin ¼'

30 1st R Drury Lane (NS) just past church on R, continue along lane, bearing sharp R at end of houses, and L at T-j 'Alsop, Fenny Bentley'

31 L after 2 km (1¼ miles)

32 Under Tissington Trail after 800 m (½ mile) then R at T-j 'Ashbourne A515; Alsop 1¾, Fenny Bentley 5' and immediately L (NS)

◀ **page 90**

14 *The Dove and the Manifold valleys*

This ride goes south along the Dove Valley, then heads for Waterhouses and the Manifold Track. It then crosses the plateau to Alstonefield and down to Milldale before joining the Tissington Trail to return to Ashbourne. There are good views west from the Clifton to Snelston Road across the Dove Valley and on the road from Hulme End to Alstonefield. Be wary of quarry traffic between Ellastone and Waterhouses.

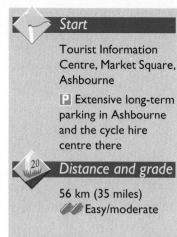

Start

Tourist Information Centre, Market Square, Ashbourne

P Extensive long-term parking in Ashbourne and the cycle hire centre there

Distance and grade

56 km (35 miles)

Easy/moderate

▼ *Dovedale*

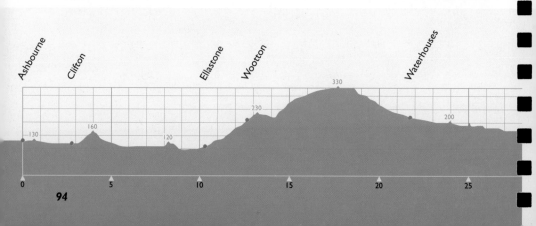

Terrain

The climb from Ellastone to Cauldon Lowe and an easier one from Hulme End to Alstonefield are followed by enjoyable descents. From Milldale up to the Tissington Trail is steep but short

Nearest railway

Uttoxeter, 19 km (12 miles) from start
Derby 22 km (14 miles) from start

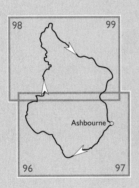

Places of interest

Dovedale and the River Dove 19
Dovedale is one of the great 'draws' of the Peak. The gorge, running south of Hartington as far as Ilam, has famous features which are mostly accessible only on foot – neither road nor bridleway runs down the bottom of the valley. The only section of the Dove Gorge which can be cycled lies between Milldale and Shining Tor

Alstonefield 18
A remote upland settlement west of the Dove, it is the meeting place of ancient paths and packhorse ways and was a market centre in late medieval times. St Peter's church has stone work from several periods, the earliest being Norman. It contains good 17th-century woodwork, including a two-decker pulpit. There are many attractive limestone cottages with mullioned windows

Refreshments

*Plenty of choice in **Ashbourne***
*Duncombe Arms, **Ellastone***
*Yew Tree Inn, **Cauldon***
*Shop, pubs and cycle hire centre at **Waterhouses***
Teas at Lea House Farm and Wettonmill along **Manifold Track**
*Manifold Valley Hotel, **Hulme End***
*George and Dragon PH, **Alstonefield***

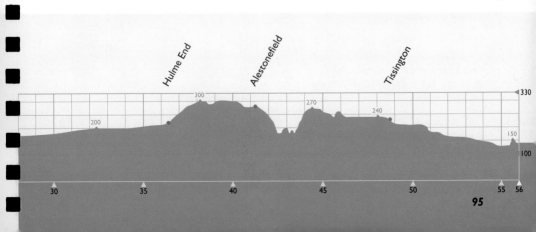

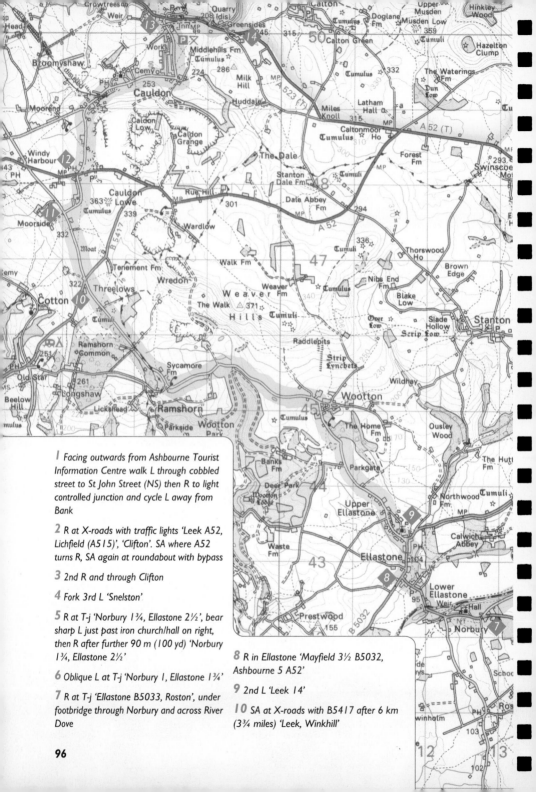

1 Facing outwards from Ashbourne Tourist Information Centre walk L through cobbled street to St John Street (NS) then R to light controlled junction and cycle L away from Bank

2 R at X-roads with traffic lights 'Leek A52, Lichfield (A515)', 'Clifton'. SA where A52 turns R, SA again at roundabout with bypass

3 2nd R and through Clifton

4 Fork 3rd L 'Snelston'

5 R at T-j 'Norbury 1¾, Ellastone 2½', bear sharp L just past iron church/hall on right, then R after further 90 m (100 yd) 'Norbury 1¾, Ellastone 2½'

6 Oblique L at T-j 'Norbury 1, Ellastone 1¾'

7 R at T-j 'Ellastone B5033, Roston', under footbridge through Norbury and across River Dove

8 R in Ellastone 'Mayfield 3½ B5032, Ashbourne 5 A52'

9 2nd L 'Leek 14'

10 SA at X-roads with B5417 after 6 km (3¾ miles) 'Leek, Winkhill'

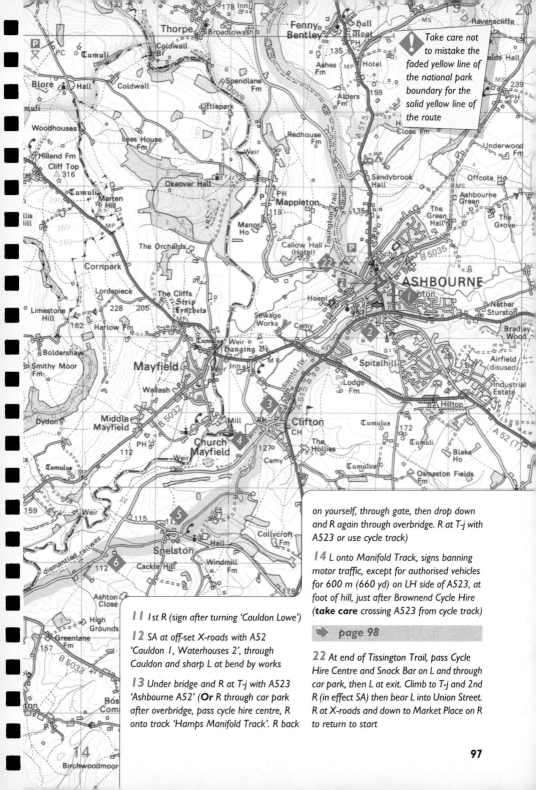

Take care not to mistake the faded yellow line of the national park boundary for the solid yellow line of the route

11 1st R (sign after turning 'Cauldon Lowe')

12 SA at off-set X-roads with A52 'Cauldon 1, Waterhouses 2', through Cauldon and sharp L at bend by works

13 Under bridge and R at T-j with A523 'Ashbourne A52' (**Or** R through car park after overbridge, pass cycle hire centre, R onto track 'Hamps Manifold Track'. R back on yourself, through gate, then drop down and R again through overbridge. R at T-j with A523 or use cycle track)

14 L onto Manifold Track, signs banning motor traffic, except for authorised vehicles for 600 m (660 yd) on LH side of A523, at foot of hill, just after Brownend Cycle Hire (**take care** crossing A523 from cycle track)

➡️ *page 98*

22 At end of Tissington Trail, pass Cycle Hire Centre and Snack Bar on L and through car park, then L at exit. Climb to T-j and 2nd R (in effect SA) then bear L into Union Street. R at X-roads and down to Market Place on R to return to start

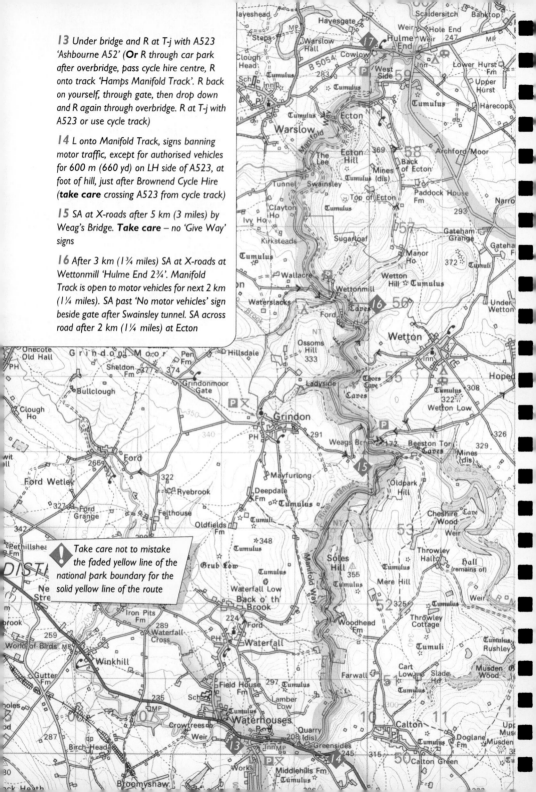

13 Under bridge and R at T-j with A523 'Ashbourne A52' (**Or** R through car park after overbridge, pass cycle hire centre, R onto track 'Hamps Manifold Track'. R back on yourself, through gate, then drop down and R again through overbridge. R at T-j with A523 or use cycle track)

14 L onto Manifold Track, signs banning motor traffic, except for authorised vehicles for 600 m (660 yd) on LH side of A523, at foot of hill, just after Brownend Cycle Hire (**take care** crossing A523 from cycle track)

15 SA at X-roads after 5 km (3 miles) by Weag's Bridge. **Take care** – no 'Give Way' signs

16 After 3 km (1¾ miles) SA at X-roads at Wettonmill 'Hulme End 2¾'. Manifold Track is open to motor vehicles for next 2 km (1¼ miles). SA past 'No motor vehicles' sign beside gate after Swainsley tunnel. SA across road after 2 km (1¼ miles) at Ecton

Take care not to mistake the faded yellow line of the national park boundary for the solid yellow line of the route

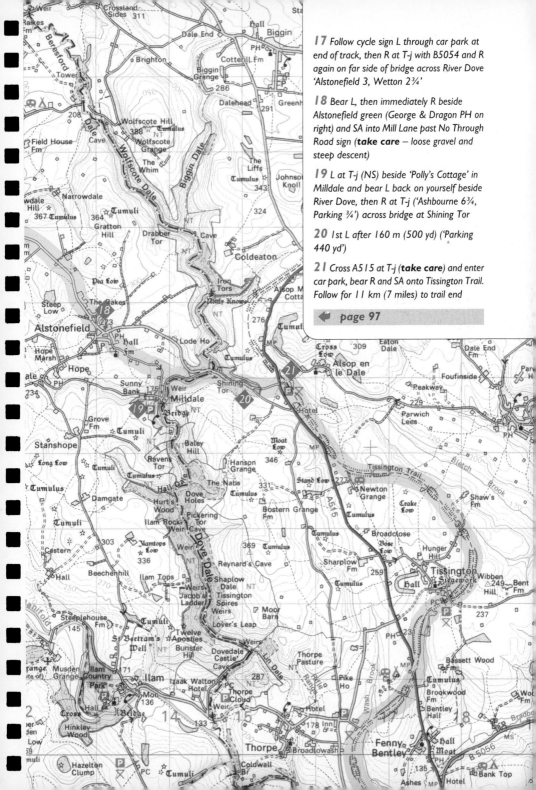

17 Follow cycle sign L through car park at end of track, then R at T-j with B5054 and R again on far side of bridge across River Dove 'Alstonefield 3, Wetton 2¾'

18 Bear L, then immediately R beside Alstonefield green (George & Dragon PH on right) and SA into Mill Lane past No Through Road sign (**take care** – loose gravel and steep descent)

19 L at T-j (NS) beside 'Polly's Cottage' in Milldale and bear L back on yourself beside River Dove, then R at T-j ('Ashbourne 6¾, Parking ¾') across bridge at Shining Tor

20 1st L after 160 m (500 yd) ('Parking 440 yd')

21 Cross A515 at T-j (**take care**) and enter car park, bear R and SA onto Tissington Trail. Follow for 11 km (7 miles) to trail end

◀ **page 97**

15 *Old Roads around Buxton*

This route explores the White Peak around Buxton. It follows the line of several old packhorse routes and turnpikes and offers excellent views on fine days. Conspicuous hills on either side of Dowel Dale – on the left bank of Upper Dovedale – are classically hill-shaped (almost unique in the Peak District). This is because they are formed from reef limestone which is harder than the carboniferous kind which underlies most of the White Peak and resisted the effects of glaciation.

Refreshments

*Plenty of choice in **Buxton**
Plenty of choice in **Longnor**
Waterloo PH at crossing of A6 west of **Taddington**
Angler's Rest PH, **Miller's Dale**
Plenty of choice in **Tideswell**
PH in **Smalldale**
Midland Hotel, **Peak Dale***

Start

Buxton Tourist Information Centre, The Crescent

P Various public car parks in Buxton

Distance and grade

42 km (26 miles)
🥾🥾🥾🥾 Moderate/ strenuous

Terrain

Unsealed former turnpike roads, grass bridleways and farm tracks. Long off-road climb out of Buxton, and shorter on-road climbs out of Dovedale, from Miller's Dale and up to Wheston. Some stretches of bridleway are deeply rutted

Nearest railway

Buxton

Buxton · Axe Edge Moor 520 · Leap Edge · Dowall Hall · Glutton Bridge · Abbotside Farm

470 · 440 · 400 · 390
320 · 320

0   5   10   15   20

Buxton 1

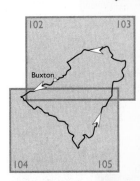

One of the centres of the Peak. It began as a spa on the boundary between the limestone and the millstone grit, where water emerged from the ground at 28° C (82° F). The Romans had a bathing station (Aquae Arnemetiae) and many routes converged on it. Mary Queen of Scots sought the cure here for her rheumatism. The town was originally around the Market Place but expanded downhill in the 18th century when the 5th Duke of Devonshire resolved to create a northern rival to Bath. The Crescent was built in the 1780s, followed by stables which were converted into the Devonshire Royal Hospital in 1859. The Pump Room opposite is now a Micrarium where you may see the universe at microscopic level, St Ann's Cliff and gardens behind and above it.

◀ *The River Wye*

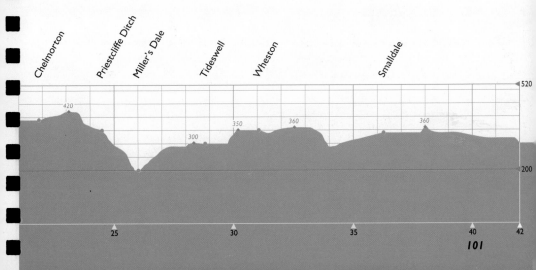

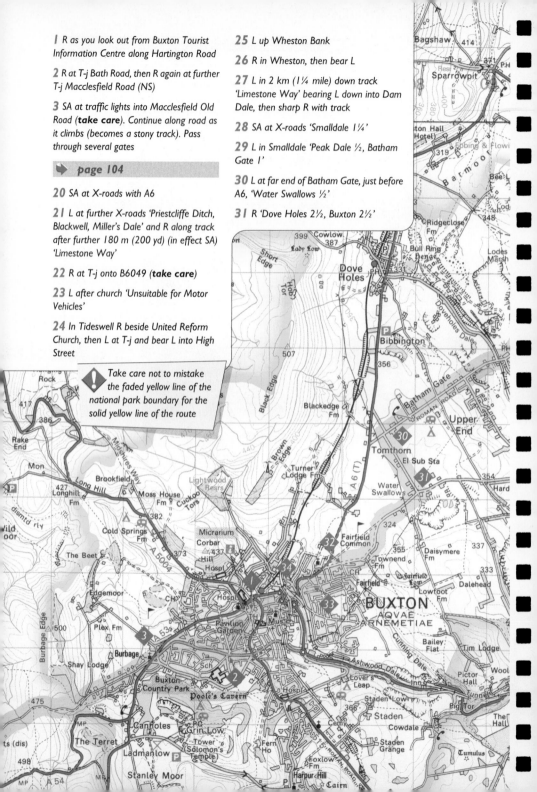

1 R as you look out from Buxton Tourist Information Centre along Hartington Road

2 R at T-j Bath Road, then R again at further T-j Macclesfield Road (NS)

3 SA at traffic lights into Macclesfield Old Road (**take care**). Continue along road as it climbs (becomes a stony track). Pass through several gates

➡ *page 104*

20 SA at X-roads with A6

21 L at further X-roads 'Priestcliffe Ditch, Blackwell, Miller's Dale' and R along track after further 180 m (200 yd) (in effect SA) 'Limestone Way'

22 R at T-j onto B6049 (**take care**)

23 L after church 'Unsuitable for Motor Vehicles'

24 In Tideswell R beside United Reform Church, then L at T-j and bear L into High Street

25 L up Wheston Bank

26 R in Wheston, then bear L

27 L in 2 km (1¼ mile) down track 'Limestone Way' bearing L down into Dam Dale, then sharp R with track

28 SA at X-roads 'Smalldale 1¼'

29 L in Smalldale 'Peak Dale ½, Batham Gate 1'

30 L at far end of Batham Gate, just before A6, 'Water Swallows ½'

31 R 'Dove Holes 2½, Buxton 2½'

! Take care not to mistake the faded yellow line of the national park boundary for the solid yellow line of the route

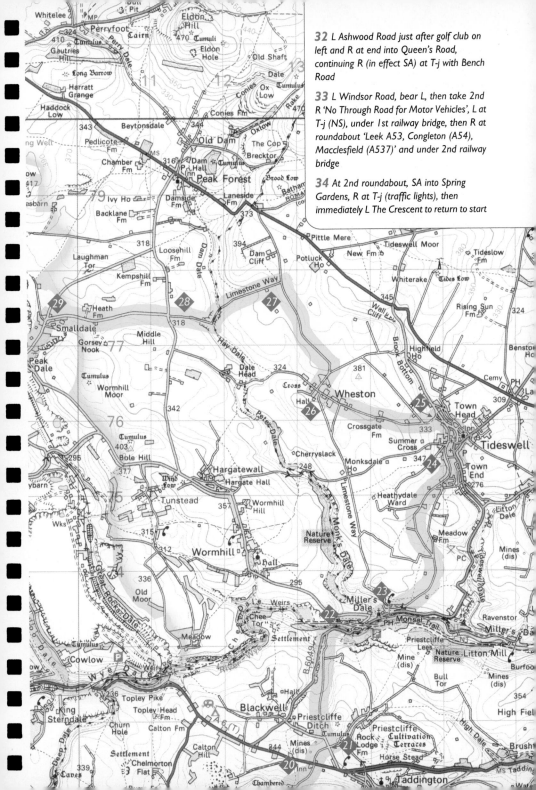

32 L Ashwood Road just after golf club on left and R at end into Queen's Road, continuing R (in effect SA) at T-j with Bench Road

33 L Windsor Road, bear L, then take 2nd R 'No Through Road for Motor Vehicles', L at T-j (NS), under 1st railway bridge, then R at roundabout 'Leek A53, Congleton (A54), Macclesfield (A537)' and under 2nd railway bridge

34 At 2nd roundabout, SA into Spring Gardens, R at T-j (traffic lights), then immediately L The Crescent to return to start

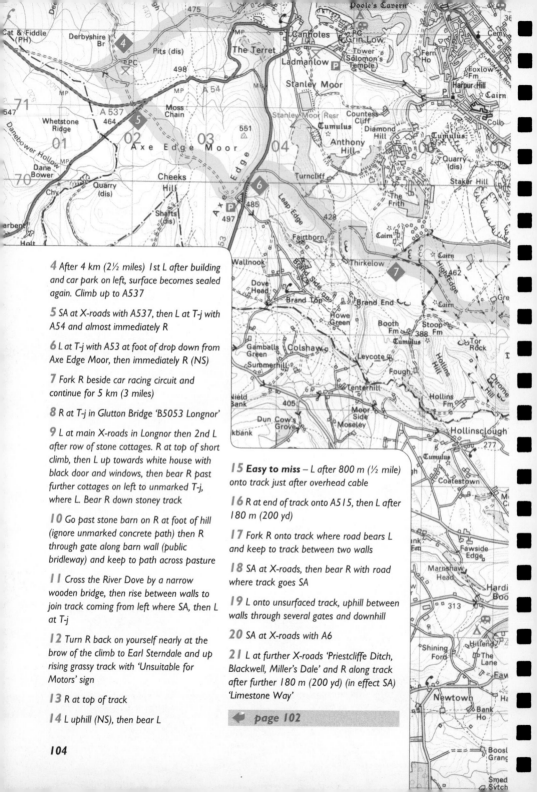

4 After 4 km (2½ miles) 1st L after building and car park on left, surface becomes sealed again. Climb up to A537

5 SA at X-roads with A537, then L at T-j with A54 and almost immediately R

6 L at T-j with A53 at foot of drop down from Axe Edge Moor, then immediately R (NS)

7 Fork R beside car racing circuit and continue for 5 km (3 miles)

8 R at T-j in Glutton Bridge 'B5053 Longnor'

9 L at main X-roads in Longnor then 2nd L after row of stone cottages. R at top of short climb, then L up towards white house with black door and windows, then bear R past further cottages on left to unmarked T-j, where L. Bear R down stoney track

10 Go past stone barn on R at foot of hill (ignore unmarked concrete path) then R through gate along barn wall (public bridleway) and keep to path across pasture

11 Cross the River Dove by a narrow wooden bridge, then rise between walls to join track coming from left where SA, then L at T-j

12 Turn R back on yourself nearly at the brow of the climb to Earl Sterndale and up rising grassy track with 'Unsuitable for Motors' sign

13 R at top of track

14 L uphill (NS), then bear L

15 **Easy to miss** – L after 800 m (½ mile) onto track just after overhead cable

16 R at end of track onto A515, then L after 180 m (200 yd)

17 Fork R onto track where road bears L and keep to track between two walls

18 SA at X-roads, then bear R with road where track goes SA

19 L onto unsurfaced track, uphill between walls through several gates and downhill

20 SA at X-roads with A6

21 L at further X-roads 'Priestcliffe Ditch, Blackwell, Miller's Dale' and R along track after further 180 m (200 yd) (in effect SA) 'Limestone Way'

← page 102

Take care not to mistake the faded yellow line of the national park boundary for the solid yellow line of the route

Around the Derwent Reservoirs

These are mainly off-road routes which join with each other to offer alternative rides from Fairholmes (between the Derwent and Ladybower reservoirs). The Upper Derwent Valley has been dammed in the course of the last hundred years and three reservoirs now fill it and the Woodlands Valley to the west. It is a popular area but the National Park has imposed traffic restrictions at the busiest times and there are many opportunities for off-road and virtually traffic-free cycling.

Start

Fairholmes Car Park

P Fairholmes National Park Information Centre and Cycle Hire Centre

Distance and grade

Route 16A 24 km (15 miles)
Easy
Route 16B 10 km (6¼ miles)
Easy/moderate

Terrain

The roads and tracks round the reservoirs are easy but the valley sides are quite steep

Nearest railway

Hope and Bamford

Refreshments

Drinks and snacks are available at Fairholmes Visitor Centre, and sometimes near the phone box below the Derwent Dam on the east side of **Ladybower Reservoir**
Ladybower Inn (on A57 east of instruction 4 on Route 16B)
The Yorkshire Bridge PH

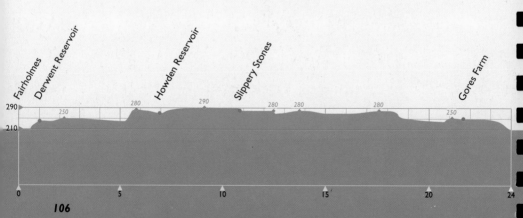

Route 16A

The Derwent Valley

The upper Derwent Valley was remote and sparsely populated when the growing demand for water in the industrial cities of the East Midlands brought about the construction of the great stone dams, to hold back the Howden and Derwent Reservoirs, in the years before the Great War. Increased need for water brought about a third, earth dam at Yorkshire Bridge, retaining Ladybower Reservoir and inaugurated by King George VI in 1945. This time, the villages of Ashop and Derwent were submerged. The two stone dams were among those used for practice flying by the RAF in preparation for the dambuster raids in the Ruhr valleys, where the dams were similar in design

◄ *Derwent Dam*

Route 16B

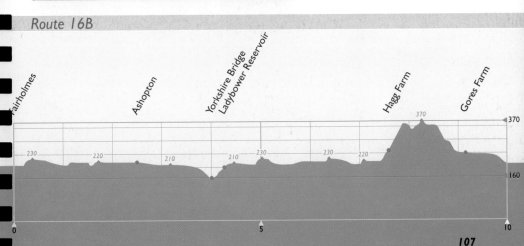

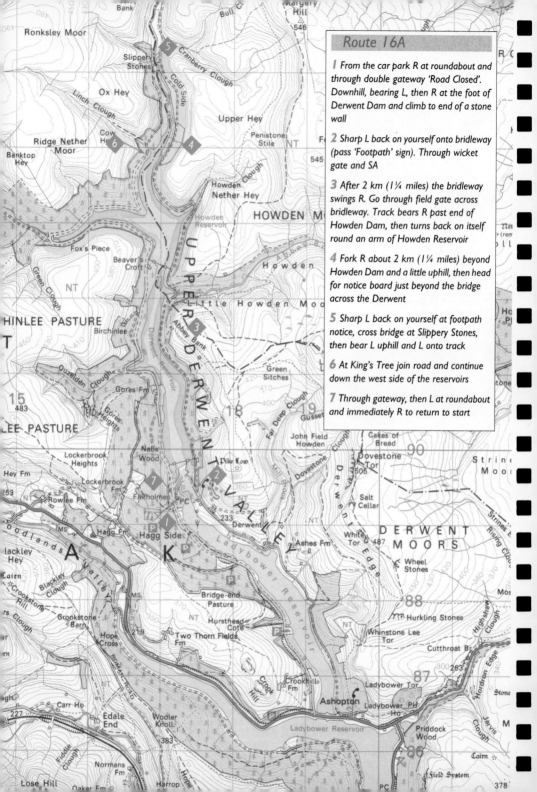

Route 16A

1 From the car park R at roundabout and through double gateway 'Road Closed'. Downhill, bearing L, then R at the foot of Derwent Dam and climb to end of a stone wall

2 Sharp L back on yourself onto bridleway (pass 'Footpath' sign). Through wicket gate and SA

3 After 2 km (1¼ miles) the bridleway swings R. Go through field gate across bridleway. Track bears R past end of Howden Dam, then turns back on itself round an arm of Howden Reservoir

4 Fork R about 2 km (1¼ miles) beyond Howden Dam and a little uphill, then head for notice board just beyond the bridge across the Derwent

5 Sharp L back on yourself at footpath notice, cross bridge at Slippery Stones, then bear L uphill and L onto track

6 At King's Tree join road and continue down the west side of the reservoirs

7 Through gateway, then L at roundabout and immediately R to return to start

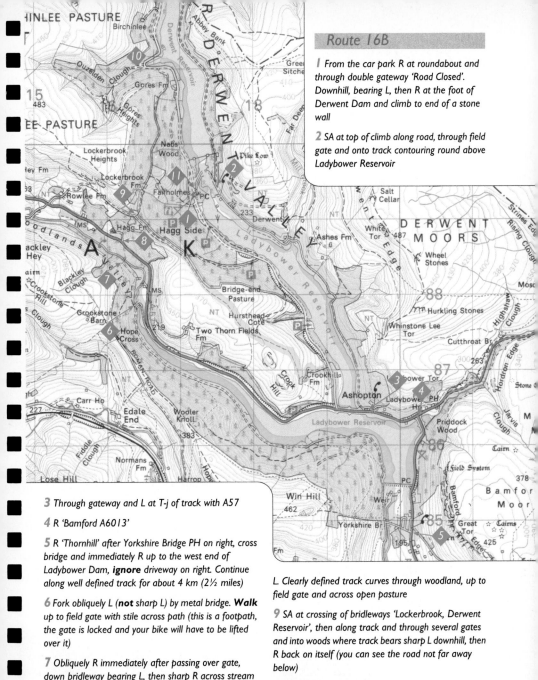

1 From the car park R at roundabout and through double gateway 'Road Closed'. Downhill, bearing L, then R at the foot of Derwent Dam and climb to end of a stone wall

2 SA at top of climb along road, through field gate and onto track contouring round above Ladybower Reservoir

3 Through gateway and L at T-j of track with A57

4 R 'Bamford A6013'

5 R 'Thornhill' after Yorkshire Bridge PH on right, cross bridge and immediately R up to the west end of Ladybower Dam, **ignore** driveway on right. Continue along well defined track for about 4 km (2½ miles)

6 Fork obliquely L (**not** sharp L) by metal bridge. **Walk** up to field gate with stile across path (this is a footpath, the gate is locked and your bike will have to be lifted over it)

7 Obliquely R immediately after passing over gate, down bridleway bearing L, then sharp R across stream and uphill again between walls

8 Through gate, across A57 up drive to Hagg Farm 'Derwent Dale 1½', then SA up track where drive turns

L. Clearly defined track curves through woodland, up to field gate and across open pasture

9 SA at crossing of bridleways 'Lockerbrook, Derwent Reservoir', then along track and through several gates and into woods where track bears sharp L downhill, then R back on itself (you can see the road not far away below)

10 R at T-j with tarmacked road (NS)

11 Through gateway, then L at roundabout and immediately R to return to the start

109

17 Houndkirk, Stanedge Pole and Abney

Mixes of quiet roads, unmaintained county roads and bridleways across moorland and rivers. On the road from Fox House towards Hathersage is Surprise View from which the valley of the Derwent and Noe rivers beyond are a magnificent sight. To the north of the road is Carl Wark, a great hill fort – it may be Iron Age, post-Roman or a mixture of both. Stanage Edge is a popular area for walkers and climbers and the track crossing it was once a packhorse way.

Refreshments

The Yorkshire Bridge PH
Plenty of choice in **Hathersage**
Station cafe, **Grindleford**
Fox House Inn
Norfolk Arms, **Ringinglow**
Several pubs and shop in **Bamford**
Traveller PH, **Brough**
Greyhound PH, **Leadmill**

Start

Hathersage Station

P Off Oddfellows Road, Hathersage

Distance and grade

35 km (22 miles)
(22 km (14 miles) if returning direct to Hathersage from instruction 11)

Moderate

Terrain

The sections from Grindleford to Fox House, off-road from Redmires up to Stanedge Pole and again from Brough to Abney need some effort and the descent of Stanage Edge needs care – none are too difficult

Nearest railway

Edale, Grindleford, Hathersage and Hope

Elevation profile — labels left to right: Hathersage, Leadmill, Grindleford, Grindleford Station, Fox House Inn, Ringinglow, Ash Cabin Flat

Elevations noted: 150, 150, 420, 370, 350, 440

Horizontal scale: 0, 5, 10, 15

Places of interest

Longshaw 2/3

The Longshaw Estate, once a shooting ground of the Manners family, is now in the hands of the National Trust. There are over 600 ha (1,500 acres) of woodland and open moor with extensive footpaths, well worth exploring

Fox House and Houndkirk 3

Houndkirk Road, rising to almost 425 m (1400 ft), used to be the turnpike route linking Grindleford and Hathersage with Sheffield and may have Roman or earlier origins. It was replaced in 1812 by the Duke of Devonshire. Fox House was constructed by a Mr Fox (a local landowner) as the destination for his constitutionals and subsequently became a staging point for coaches. Charlotte Brontë is claimed to have had Fox House in mind as the alighting point for Jane Eyre on her flight to Morton/Hathersage

▼ Bole Hill, Eyam Moor

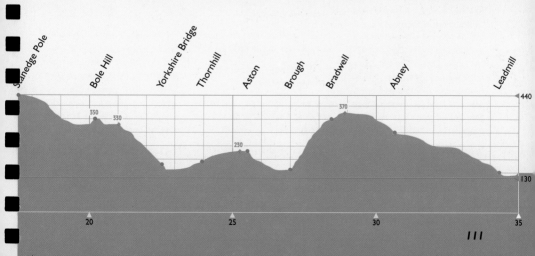

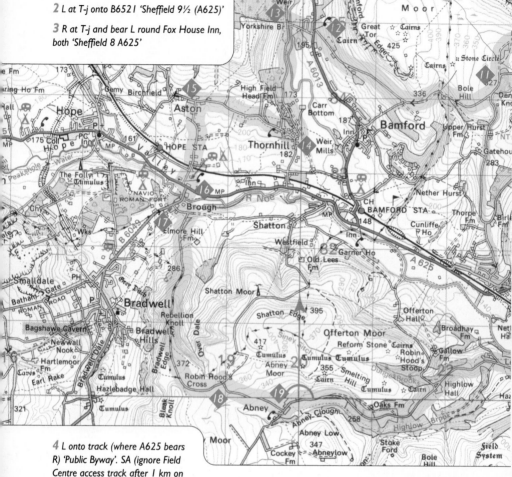

1 L from Hathersage Station road exit onto B6001, passing under the railway bridge and SA to Grindleford

2 L at T-j onto B6521 'Sheffield 9½ (A625)'

3 R at T-j and bear L round Fox House Inn, both 'Sheffield 8 A625'

4 L onto track (where A625 bears R) 'Public Byway'. SA (ignore Field Centre access track after 1 km on left) and pass through wicket gate by locked field gate. Bear slightly R and ignore footpath on left. Cross a bridleway and uphill short distance. Cross stream (parapet on the R only) and head for another wicket gate by field gate. Continue SA and downhill

5 L onto road

6 L at T-j opposite Norfolk Arms PH in Ringinglow, then immediately R into Fulwood Lane

7 L at T-j Brown Hills Lane and sharp R after 365 m (400 yd)

8 L at further T-j and rise past the Redmires Reservoirs

9 At end of tarmac, R uphill beside wall along track 'Public Byway', to Stanedge Pole

10 Bear R after pole along well defined track beside fence R (surface deteriorates). At fork bear L, descending along track

11 SA where track meets road below Stanage Edge, then R after 180 m (200 yd) 'Ladybower' (**Or** for short cut back to Hathersage SA. Outside Hathersage L into Jagger's Lane, then L at T-j and R onto B6001 'Grindleford 3, Baslow 5' to return to station

12 L at T-j with A6013, then immediately R 'Thornhill' to cross River Derwent

13 Bear L immediately after bridge

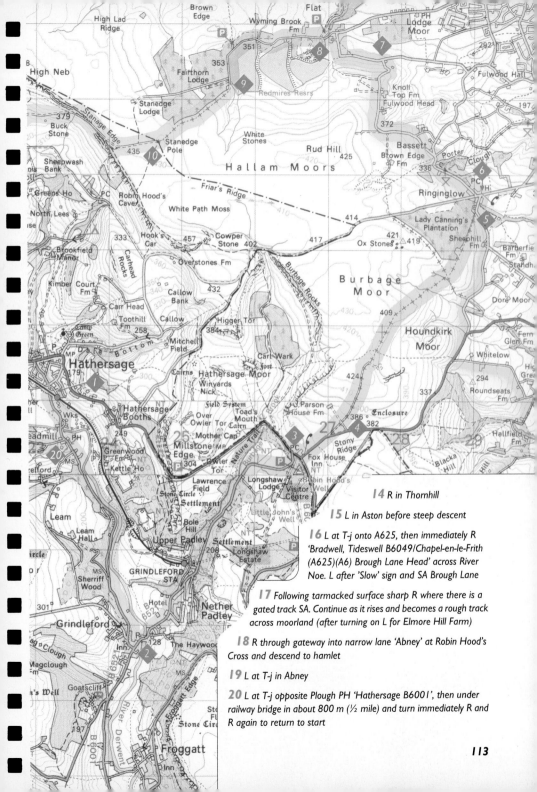

14 R in Thornhill

15 L in Aston before steep descent

16 L at T-j onto A625, then immediately R 'Bradwell, Tideswell B6049/Chapel-en-le-Frith (A625)(A6) Brough Lane Head' across River Noe. L after 'Slow' sign and SA Brough Lane

17 Following tarmacked surface sharp R where there is a gated track SA. Continue as it rises and becomes a rough track across moorland (after turning on L for Elmore Hill Farm)

18 R through gateway into narrow lane 'Abney' at Robin Hood's Cross and descend to hamlet

19 L at T-j in Abney

20 L at T-j opposite Plough PH 'Hathersage B6001', then under railway bridge in about 800 m (½ mile) and turn immediately R and R again to return to start

18 From Castleton to Great Hucklow, returning by the River Noe

A short route passing Mam Tor, the shivering mountain, that is made up of alternating layers of shale and firmer rock. Mam Tor has had repeated landslips and the old turnpike road closed to motor traffic twenty years ago following major subsidence. The ride continues over Old Moor to the Hucklows and Offerton – a small hamlet with some fascinating stone houses dating from the 16th and 17th centuries.

Start

Tourist Information Centre, Castleton

P Pay and display car park on north side of A625 in Castleton

Distance and grade

28 km (17 miles)
Moderate

Terrain

The start of the route over the old Mam Tor road is not hard but you may need to dismount to pass some of the landslides. The high level stretch from Mam Tor to Offerton is easy, though you should keep a look out for quarry traffic. The descent from Offerton, on large cobbles, requires care in wet weather

Refreshments

Plenty of choice in **Castleton**
Queen Anne PH, **Great Hucklow**
Traveller PH, **Brough**
Pubs, cafes and tea rooms in **Hope**

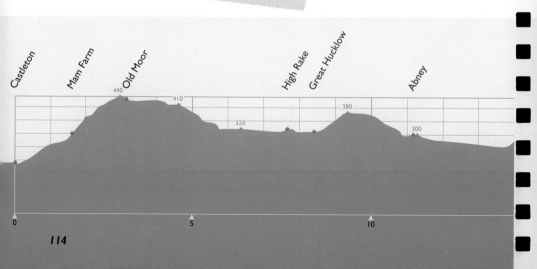

Nearest railway

Edale, Grindleford,
Hathersage and Hope

Places of interest

Castleton 1

Here the Normans created their power
centre in the Peak, and the remains of
Peveril Castle still dominates the village.
Later the extraction of minerals became
the principal activity and several old mines
now complement the natural caverns open
to the public. One of the major 'honeypots'
of the National Park

▼ Near Mam Tor

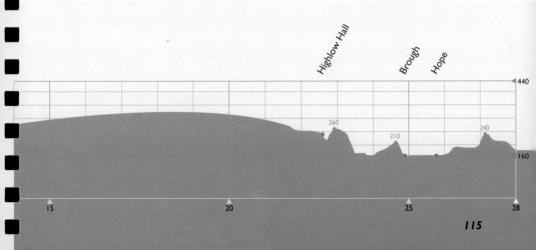

Highlow Hall

Brough

Hope

440

260

210

240

160

15   20   25   28

115

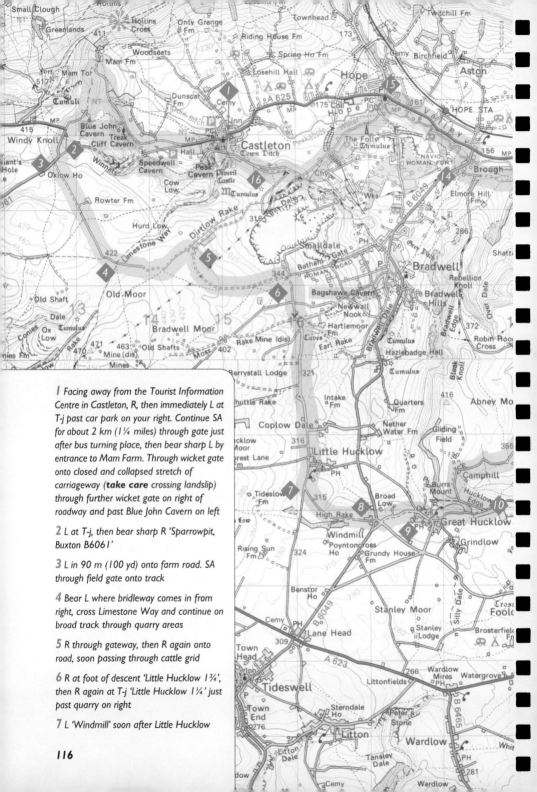

1 Facing away from the Tourist Information Centre in Castleton, R, then immediately L at T-j past car park on your right. Continue SA for about 2 km (1¼ miles) through gate just after bus turning place, then bear sharp L by entrance to Mam Farm. Through wicket gate onto closed and collapsed stretch of carriageway (**take care** crossing landslip) through further wicket gate on right of roadway and past Blue John Cavern on left

2 L at T-j, then bear sharp R 'Sparrowpit, Buxton B6061'

3 L in 90 m (100 yd) onto farm road. SA through field gate onto track

4 Bear L where bridleway comes in from right, cross Limestone Way and continue on broad track through quarry areas

5 R through gateway, then R again onto road, soon passing through cattle grid

6 R at foot of descent 'Little Hucklow 1¾', then R again at T-j 'Little Hucklow 1¼' just past quarry on right

7 L 'Windmill' soon after Little Hucklow

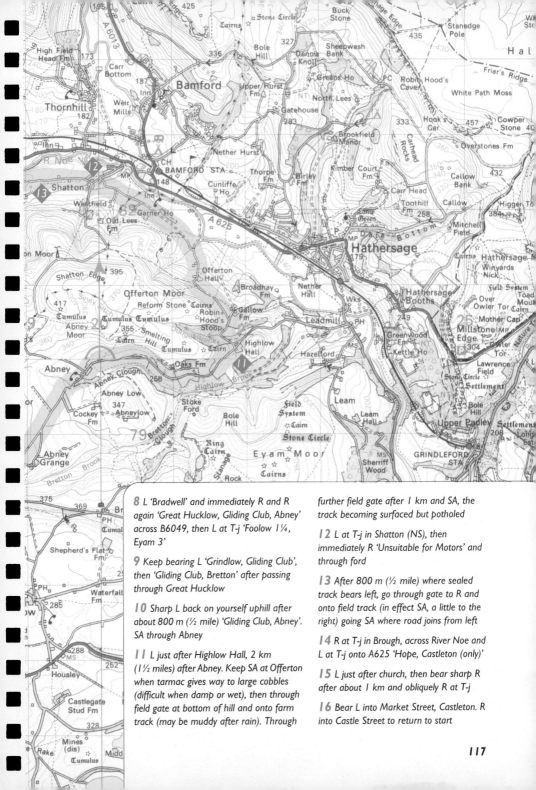

8 L 'Bradwell' and immediately R and R again 'Great Hucklow, Gliding Club, Abney' across B6049, then L at T-j 'Foolow 1¼, Eyam 3'

9 Keep bearing L 'Grindlow, Gliding Club', then 'Gliding Club, Bretton' after passing through Great Hucklow

10 Sharp L back on yourself uphill after about 800 m (½ mile) 'Gliding Club, Abney'. SA through Abney

11 L just after Highlow Hall, 2 km (1½ miles) after Abney. Keep SA at Offerton when tarmac gives way to large cobbles (difficult when damp or wet), then through field gate at bottom of hill and onto farm track (may be muddy after rain). Through

further field gate after 1 km and SA, the track becoming surfaced but potholed

12 L at T-j in Shatton (NS), then immediately R 'Unsuitable for Motors' and through ford

13 After 800 m (½ mile) where sealed track bears left, go through gate to R and onto field track (in effect SA, a little to the right) going SA where road joins from left

14 R at T-j in Brough, across River Noe and L at T-j onto A625 'Hope, Castleton (only)'

15 L just after church, then bear sharp R after about 1 km and obliquely R at T-j

16 Bear L into Market Street, Castleton. R into Castle Street to return to start

From Langsett to Low Bradfield

An exploration of the countryside north of the Loxley Valley, encompassing more deep valleys, moorland, woods and reservoirs. The chief points of interest are the views from the high moorland roads. This route can be linked with Route 8, for a strenuous circuit, joining at Low Bradfield

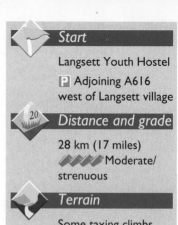

Start

Langsett Youth Hostel

P Adjoining A616 west of Langsett village

Distance and grade

28 km (17 miles)
Moderate/ strenuous

Terrain

Some taxing climbs from Ewden Bridge, up to High Bradfield, and between Broomhead Reservoir and

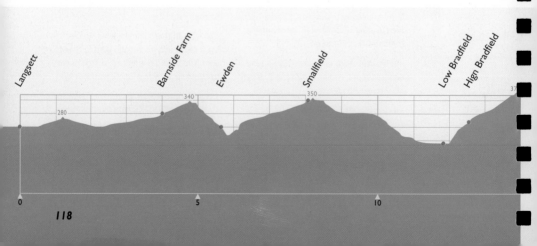

Bolsterstone, however, long sections either roughly follow contours or run downhill. The roads are fairly quiet but the steepness of the hills means that low gears and good brakes are needed

Nearest railway

Penistone (6 km)
4 miles from Langsett,
3km (2 miles) from
Cranberry Farm

Places of interest

Broomhead Hall 4
An early 19th-century building in Tudor style, downhill to the left after Ewden Bridge

Midhopestones 19
The tiny church here, St James', is a contrast with the edifice at High Bradfield. It has relics of an earlier age in its boxed pews with parishioners' names and west gallery. A Queen Anne building, with Jacobean pulpit. Nearby is an oddly curious house, described as both homely and Palladian at the same time. Built with a three bay, three storey, pedimented central section and lower, half pedimented wings

Refreshments

Waggon and Horses PH, cafe and shop, **Langsett**
Old Horns PH, **High Bradfield**
Castle Inn and shop, **Bolsterstone**
Midhopestones Arms, **Midhopestones**

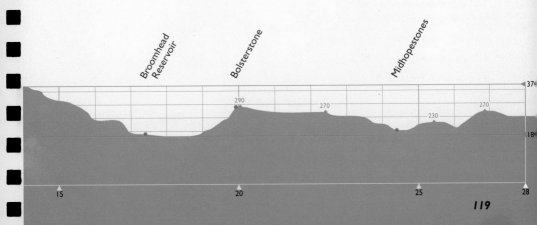

1 From Langsett Youth Hostel L at A616 (**take care**) then R at Waggon and Horses PH 'Strines, Derwentwater' and cross top of dam

2 Sharp bend R 'Strines, Derwentwater' and continue to bear L along road

3 R at T-j 'Strines, Derwentwater' shortly after forest ends on left. Take road to right, uphill over ridge, then descend to Ewden Bridge and climb (steeply at first)

4 Ignore turning L for Wigtwizzle, continue SA

5 Bear R diagonally uphill along unfenced road

6 L 'Bradfield, Dungworth' as road crosses ridge and contour L along mostly unfenced road

7 R at T-j downhill along ridge road to Low Bradfield and Agden Reservoir

8 L at T-j above Low Bradfield and immediately up steep hill

9 L at T-j in High Bradfield, Brown House Lane 'Bolsterstone 4¾, Midhopestones 5¾'

10 Fork R 'Midhopestones 5¼'

11 L at T-j with milestone (**take care –** sharp bends on steep hill)

12 SA at X-roads and descend towards reservoir

13 Keep SA to head of reservoir

14 Bear R round head of reservoir and R at T-j 'Bolsterstone 2, Stocksbridge 4', then bear L uphill, away from reservoir

15 L in Bolsterstone by Castle Inn 'Stocksbridge 1½, Midhopestones 2½'

16 L, then fork R in about 400 m (¼ mile)

17 Fork L at grass triangle (NS)

18 Obliquely R 'Penistone 3, Midhopestones ½'

19 L by Midhopestones Arms 'Upper Midhope 1½', then R at T-j at Upper Midhope 'Langsett ½' to return across dam to the start

Take care not to mistake the faded yellow line of the national park boundary for the solid yellow line of the route

The White Peak

Through old mining villages in the White Peak, between the Derwent and Dove rivers, southwest of Bakewell. Quarrying is still important around Brassington and Parwich. There is little surface water in the area but the River Lathkill, below Over Haddon and the River Bradford at Alport offer delightful riverside walks and views.

Start

Tourist Information Centre, Bakewell Market Place

P Extensive (but busy) pay car parking in Bakewell. Car parks also at Over Haddon and along the Tissington Trail

Distance and grade

52 km (32 miles)

Easy/moderate

Terrain

Several sections on undulating tableland and a comfortable ascent from Parwich up to Biggin. Climbs out of the valleys of the River Wye (from Bakewell) and the River Bradford (from Alport) have sharp pitches

◀ Lathkill Dale

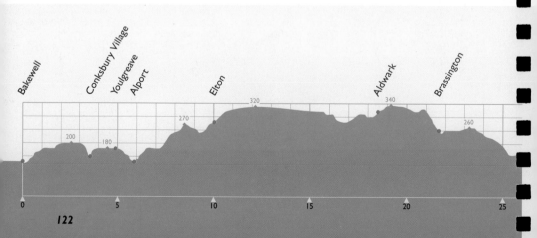

Nearest railway

Buxton, 14 km (9 miles)
from Parsley Hay
Matlock, 10 km
(6 miles) from Elton

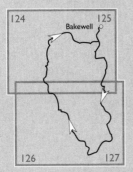

Places of interest

Bakewell 1

A busy town with a market on Mondays,
Bakewell was one of the traditional
administrative centres of Derbyshire and is
now the largest town and site of the main
offices of the Peak National Park. Past
Dukes of Rutland tried, but failed, to make
it a spa town like Buxton. Bakeries vie for
the right to be the only original source of
the Bakewell Pudding – the result, it seems,
of a cook getting things wrong when making
a jam tart at the Rutland Arms

Lathkill Dale 3

One of the larger parts of the Derbyshire
Dales National Nature Reserve and the one
most accessible to the public.
There is no cycle access
within the reserve but it is
well worth exploring on foot.
There is an information centre
at Over Haddon

Refreshments

Plenty of choice in **Bakewell**
Plenty of choice in **Youlgreave**
Cafe and PH in **Elton**
Pubs in **Brassington** and **Parwich**
Snacks at **Parsley Hay**
Old Smithy and Village Stores tea rooms and
Bull's Head PH, in **Monyash**
Yew Tree tearoom, Uncle Geoff's Diner and
Craft Centre in **Over Haddon**

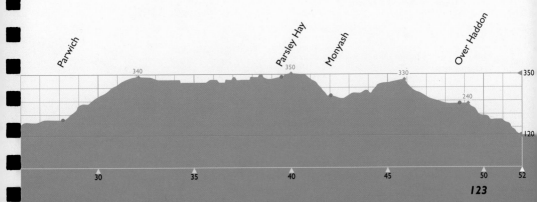

1 From Bakewell Tourist Information Centre along Bridge Street towards Rutland Arms, L at roundabout Matlock Street and immediately R King Street ('B5055 Monyash 5')

2 3rd L Yeld Road

3 L after crossing River Lathkill at Conksbury Bridge 'Youlgreave ¾'

4 L at T-j in Youlgreave (George PH on L, church SA) 'Alport ¾, Bakewell 4½'

5 R at foot of hill entering Alport, after crossing River Lathkill again. Bear L, then R at T-j (NS) and cross River Bradford

6 Sharp L at T-j 'Elton'

7 R Moor Lane in Elton

➡ **page 126**

21 After passing through cutting and joining High Peak Trail go past gate and turn back on yourself R, pass Parsley Hay Cycle Hire Centre and through car park. Turn L at exit, L again at T-j with A515, and immediately R (**take care**)

22 SA at X-roads in Monyash, then 1st R

23 R at T-j after (1½ miles) 'Ashford 2, Bakewell 3'. **Ignore** 1st junction on left 'Ashford 1'

24 R onto stony track (clump of trees at fork)

25 SA at X-roads with B5055 'Over Haddon, Lathkilldale 1½'

26 R just after 30 mph sign on entering Over Haddon (parking sign). Bear L, L again beside Over Haddon Craft Centre, then R on leaving village 'Youlgreave 2½ (**not** SA 'Bakewell 2')

27 L at T-j 'Bakewell 1½'

28 R at T-j to return to start by reverse of outward route

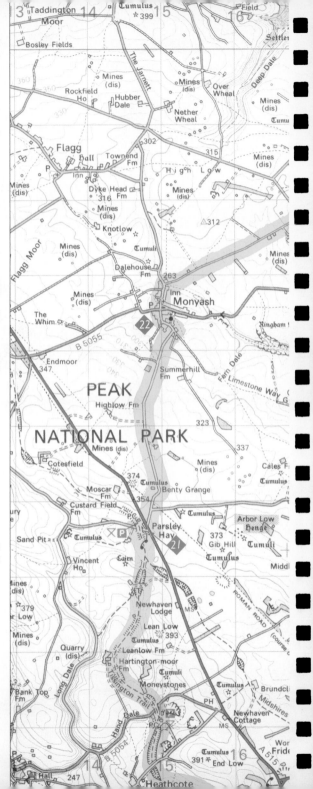

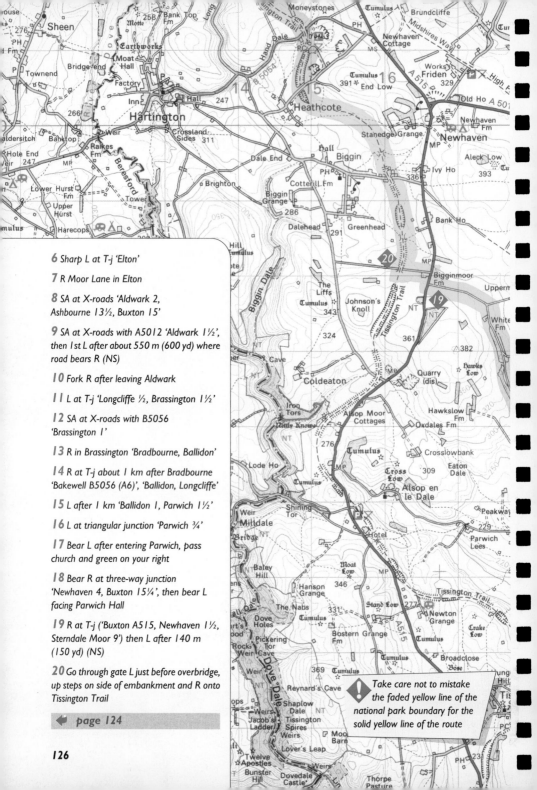

6 Sharp L at T-j 'Elton'

7 R Moor Lane in Elton

8 SA at X-roads 'Aldwark 2, Ashbourne 13½, Buxton 15'

9 SA at X-roads with A5012 'Aldwark 1½', then 1st L after about 550 m (600 yd) where road bears R (NS)

10 Fork R after leaving Aldwark

11 L at T-j 'Longcliffe ½, Brassington 1½'

12 SA at X-roads with B5056 'Brassington 1'

13 R in Brassington 'Bradbourne, Ballidon'

14 R at T-j about 1 km after Bradbourne 'Bakewell B5056 (A6)', 'Ballidon, Longcliffe'

15 L after 1 km 'Ballidon 1, Parwich 1½'

16 L at triangular junction 'Parwich ¾'

17 Bear L after entering Parwich, pass church and green on your right

18 Bear R at three-way junction 'Newhaven 4, Buxton 15¼', then bear L facing Parwich Hall

19 R at T-j ('Buxton A515, Newhaven 1½, Sterndale Moor 9') then L after 140 m (150 yd) (NS)

20 Go through gate L just before overbridge, up steps on side of embankment and R onto Tissington Trail

← **page 124**

126

! Take care not to mistake the faded yellow line of the national park boundary for the solid yellow line of the route

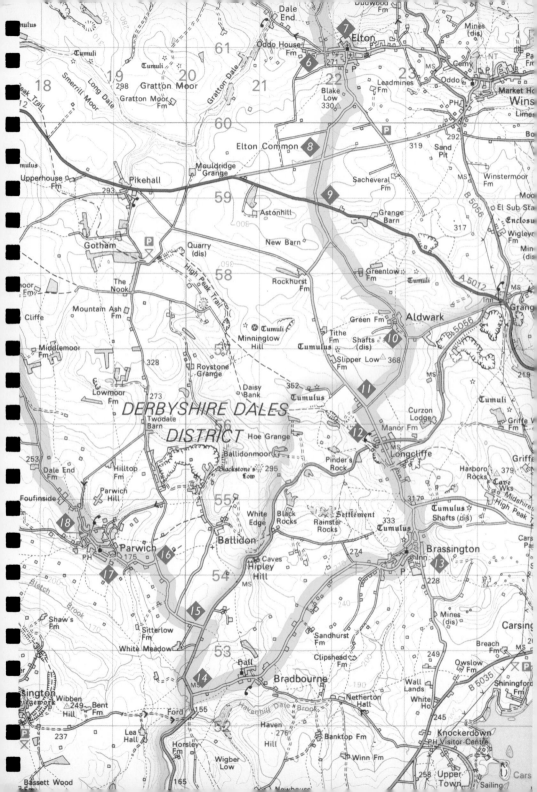

The Wye Valley and Chatsworth

A fairly short ride, packed full of interest, over country that deserves some time for exploration. The stretch from Miller's Dale to Monsal Head through the upper Wye Valley is delightful. Chatsworth and the return through the woods to Bakewell provide further sources of pleasure.

Start

Bakewell Tourist Information Office, Market Place

P Extensive parking in Bakewell (often busy)

Distance and grade

38 km (24 miles)
Easy/moderate

Terrain

A variety of terrains is encountered. The route from Bakewell to Shelton and Taddington needs an effort. There is a climb up the northern flank of the valley followed by a sharp descent and another strenuous climb to Monsal Head. The off-road route between Chatsworth and Haddon is not difficult, but may need care when wet or muddy

▲ *Miller's and Monsal Dales from Monsal Head*

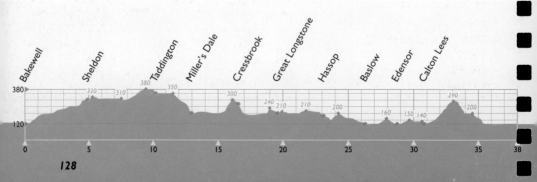

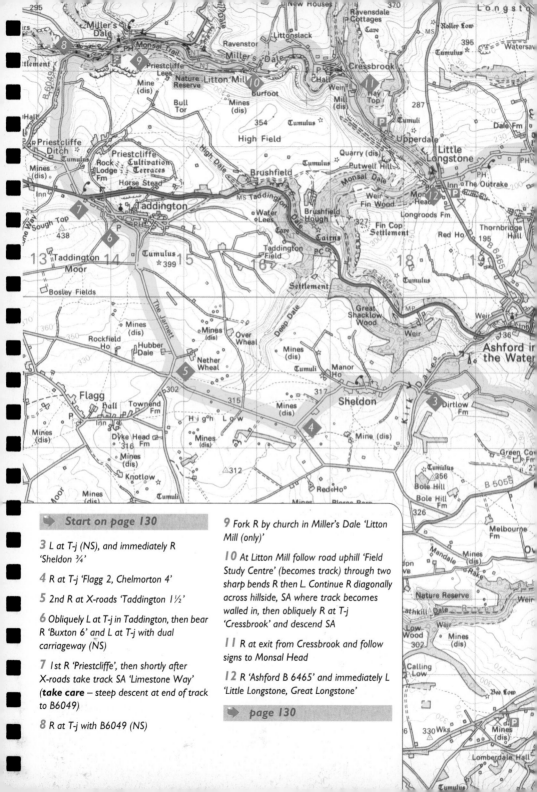

⮕ **Start on page 130**

3 L at T-j (NS), and immediately R 'Sheldon ¾'

4 R at T-j 'Flagg 2, Chelmorton 4'

5 2nd R at X-roads 'Taddington 1½'

6 Obliquely L at T-j in Taddington, then bear R 'Buxton 6' and L at T-j with dual carriageway (NS)

7 1st R 'Priestcliffe', then shortly after X-roads take track SA 'Limestone Way' (**take care** – steep descent at end of track to B6049)

8 R at T-j with B6049 (NS)

9 Fork R by church in Miller's Dale 'Litton Mill (only)'

10 At Litton Mill follow road uphill 'Field Study Centre' (becomes track) through two sharp bends R then L. Continue R diagonally across hillside, SA where track becomes walled in, then obliquely R at T-j 'Cressbrook' and descend SA

11 R at exit from Cressbrook and follow signs to Monsal Head

12 R 'Ashford B 6465' and immediately L 'Little Longstone, Great Longstone'

⮕ **page 130**

Places of interest

Monsal Dale 12
Monsal Dale is the part of the Wye Valley which stretches to the south of the old railway viaduct on your right as you climb up to Monsal Head. There is no road through this part of the valley, only footpaths, but they give access to marvellous scenery. Litton and Cressbrook Mills took pauper apprentices from London in the 18th and 19th centuries. It seems that those who were sent to Cressbrook found conditions less Dickensian than their colleagues at Litton Mill

Haddon Hall 20/21
A romantic, English country house above the left bank of the River Wye and its meadows with a wonderful view south towards Over Haddon that seemingly hangs in the air some 150 m (500 ft) higher. The house dates from the 12th to 16th centuries. It was restored with an eye on historical accuracy earlier this century and contains much material from medieval and Tudor times

Refreshments

*Plenty of choice in **Bakewell***
*Cock and Pullett PH, **Sheldon***
*Waterloo PH (just off route on A6 west of **Taddington**)*
*Angler's Rest PH, **Miller's Dale***
*Refreshments near **Litton Mill** and **Cressbrook Mill***
*Tea rooms and Inn, **Monsal Head***
*Pack Horse Inn, **Little Longstone***
*The Crispin, **Great Longstone***

Nearest railway

Matlock 13 km (8 miles) from Bakewell
Buxton 10 km (6 miles) from Taddington

1 From Bakewell Tourist Information Centre along Bridge Street towards Rutland Arms, L at roundabout Matlock Street and immediately R King Street ('B5055 Monyash 5')

2 2nd R uphill 'Ashford 2'

 page 129

13 L Church Lane 'Rowland, Hassop' in Great Longstone

14 Obliquely L at T-j in Hassop 'Hathersage B6001', then 1st R 'Baslow 2'

15 R at T-j (NS) then R at T-j with A619 (in effect SA) 'Bakewell A619, Rowsley B6012' 'Chatsworth'

16 SA for off-road route

17 Fork R 'Calton Lees, Car Park'. Pass car park and bear R. Cross drives to left and right and continue SA up unsealed track (NS). Through gateway with notice to cyclists, then zigzag R and L uphill and SA between two houses onto unsurfaced track

18 Through field gate and turn L (from here the route is well waymarked) along edge of field. Through gateway L along track (bearing L then R) and turn obliquely L where a gap in the turf resembling a plough-marked footpath leaves the track. Climb towards gate ahead

19 Through two field gates, then R along wall and bear L on grassy section of track. Through gateposts, then L (the path is both waymarked and well defined, but at a bend R becomes wider and softer). Turn sharp L beside Haddon Estate Wildlife Trail board, then shortly fork R downhill (waymark sign) and follow clearly defined path to meeting of four bridleways

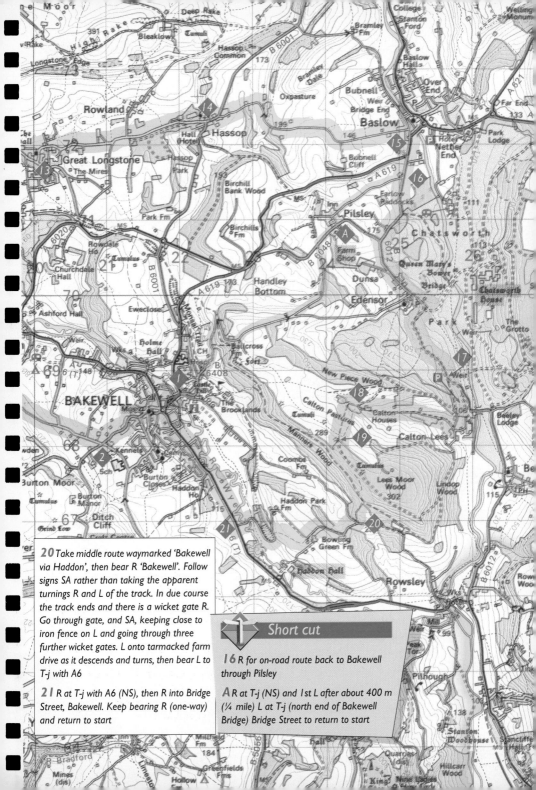

20 Take middle route waymarked 'Bakewell via Haddon', then bear R 'Bakewell'. Follow signs SA rather than taking the apparent turnings R and L of the track. In due course the track ends and there is a wicket gate R. Go through gate, and SA, keeping close to iron fence on L and going through three further wicket gates. L onto tarmacked farm drive as it descends and turns, then bear L to T-j with A6

21 R at T-j with A6 (NS), then R into Bridge Street, Bakewell. Keep bearing R (one-way) and return to start

Short cut

16 R for on-road route back to Bakewell through Pilsley

A R at T-j (NS) and 1st L after about 400 m (¼ mile) L at T-j (north end of Bakewell Bridge) Bridge Street to return to start

22 From Matlock to Monyash

A fine ride offering a variety of cycling. First the route runs upstream, above the Derwent and Wye valleys, then along the Monsal Trail. The return takes you over the open landscape of the White Peak plateau, giving extensive views of distant horizons, while passing through old mining villages.

▼ *Sheepwash Bridge, Ashford in the Water*

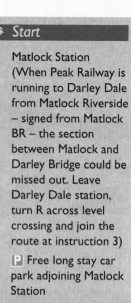

Start

Matlock Station (When Peak Railway is running to Darley Dale from Matlock Riverside – signed from Matlock BR – the section between Matlock and Darley Bridge could be missed out. Leave Darley Dale station, turn R across level crossing and join the route at instruction 3)

P Free long stay car park adjoining Matlock Station

Distance and grade

48 km (30 miles)

Moderate

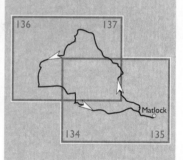

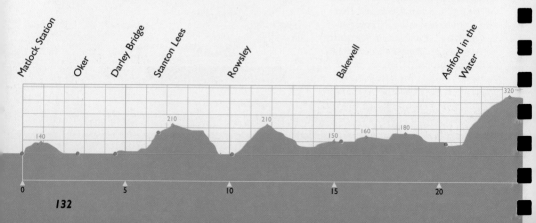

Matlock Station — Oker — Darley Bridge — Stanton Lees — Rowsley — Bakewell — Ashford in the Water

Terrain

Effort is required for the climbs out of the valleys – from Rowsley to Stanton Lees and particularly up Kirk Dale

Nearest railway

Matlock

Refreshments

*Country Gallery at **Caudwell's Mill***
*Plenty of choice in **Bakewell***
*Cottage Tea Room and shops at **Ashford in the Water***
*Bull's Head PH, **Monyash***
*Cafe and PH at **Elton***
*Pubs in **Winster***
*Plenty of choice in **Matlock***

Places of interest

Darley Dale 3
12th-century St Helen's Church has stained glass by Burne-Jones and the weatherworn remains of a great yew tree in its graveyard. There is a handsome 15th-century bridge across the Derwent. Just off the A6 are the Derbyshire Museum and Art Centre and the Working Carriage Museum

Stanton 4/5 *(just off the route)*
Stanton Moor has more than seventy barrows, cairns and other ancient relics, including the Nine Ladies – a prehistoric standing-stone circle. There are other farm houses from the 16th and 17th centuries

Arbor Low 16 *(signed R after about 1·km)*
The major neolithic site of the Peak and dubbed the 'Stonehenge of the North', Arbor Low is 46 limestone slabs lying on a circular bank surrounded by a ditch over 240 m (800 ft) in circumference and four stones in the centre. Access is by concessionary path, and there is an honesty box. There are many other prehistoric remains in the vicinity

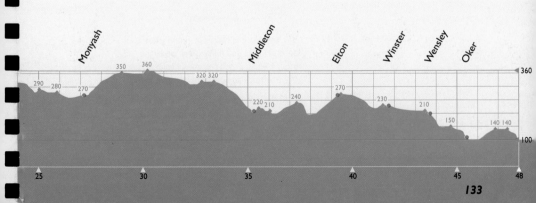

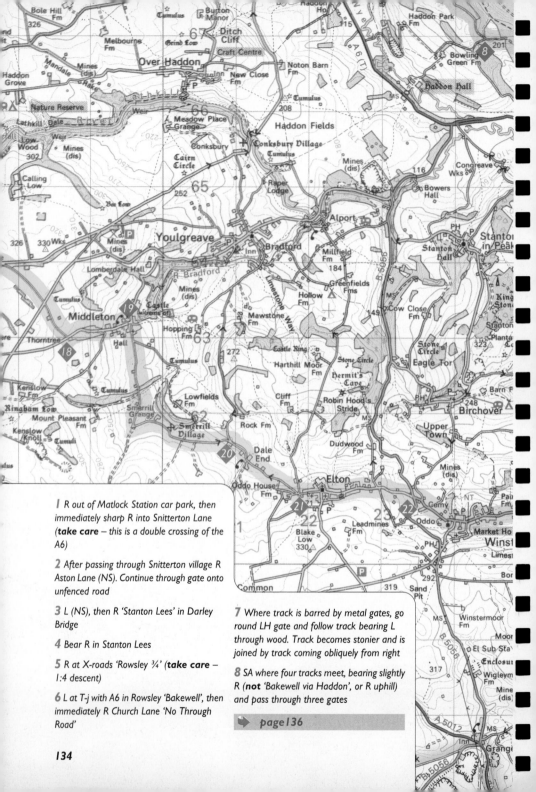

1 R out of Matlock Station car park, then immediately sharp R into Snitterton Lane (**take care** – this is a double crossing of the A6)

2 After passing through Snitterton village R Aston Lane (NS). Continue through gate onto unfenced road

3 L (NS), then R 'Stanton Lees' in Darley Bridge

4 Bear R in Stanton Lees

5 R at X-roads 'Rowsley ¾' (**take care** – 1:4 descent)

6 L at T-j with A6 in Rowsley 'Bakewell', then immediately R Church Lane 'No Through Road'

7 Where track is barred by metal gates, go round LH gate and follow track bearing L through wood. Track becomes stonier and is joined by track coming obliquely from right

8 SA where four tracks meet, bearing slightly R (**not** 'Bakewell via Haddon', or R uphill) and pass through three gates

➡ *page 136*

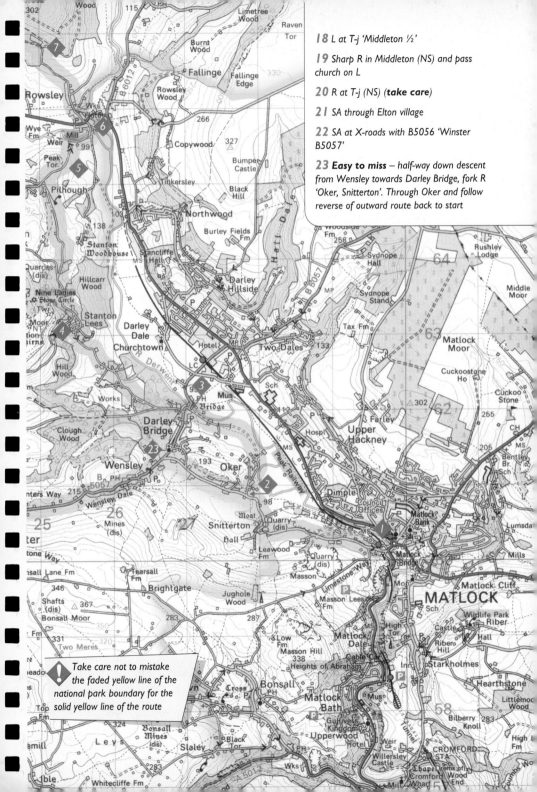

18 L at T-j 'Middleton ½'

19 Sharp R in Middleton (NS) and pass church on L

20 R at T-j (NS) (**take care**)

21 SA through Elton village

22 SA at X-roads with B5056 'Winster B5057'

23 **Easy to miss** – half-way down descent from Wensley towards Darley Bridge, fork R 'Oker, Snitterton'. Through Oker and follow reverse of outward route back to start

Take care not to mistake the faded yellow line of the national park boundary for the solid yellow line of the route

7 Where track is barred by metal gates, go round LH gate and follow track bearing L through wood. Track becomes stonier and is joined by track coming obliquely from right

8 SA where four tracks meet, bearing slightly R (**not** 'Bakewell via Haddon', or R uphill) and pass through three gates

9 R up path on side of embankment after old railway viaduct, past wooden gate (marked 2 on gatepost) and L onto Monsal Trail

10 In about 5 km (3 miles) go under overbridge soon after passing footpath (signed across trail) and enter Great Longstone Station. Carry bike up steps on far RH side of bridge, then R at exit onto road (this is the last cycle access for the Monsal Trail)

11 SA at X-roads, then bear L into Ashford in the Water (NS) and L again at T-j 'Bakewell, Matlock' (in effect SA) along main street

12 Where road bears L, enter bay marked 'Buses Only' and **walk** SA across footbridge onto A6. On road R, then 1st L (NS)

13 R at T-j at summit (NS)

14 1st L (NS)

15 L at T-j 'Monyash', then SA at X-roads into Rake Road and bear R 'Newhaven 4, Youlgreave 6' ('White Peak scenic route')

16 L 'Youlgreave, Lathkilldale', 'Arbor Low', 'White Peak scenic route' just before T-j with A515

17 R after 3 km (1¾ miles) 'White Peak scenic route' and SA at X-roads 'Middleton 1'

18 L at T-j 'Middleton ½'

19 Sharp R in Middleton (NS) and pass church on left

◄ page 135

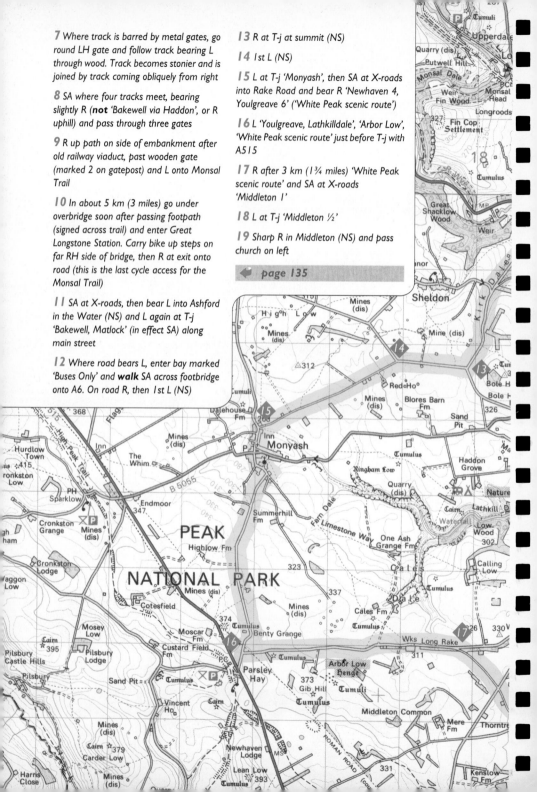

23 Rowarth, the Etherow and Werneth Low

A short ride exploring the land to the west of the A624. The countryside is often very quiet, but the roads from Marple to Mottram can be busier than their width suggests. There are good views between Simmondley and Charlesworth, from Monks' Road and from Werneth Low.

Start

Glossop Station

P Several public car parks in Glossop. Etherow Country Park at Compstall

Distance and grade

34 km (21 miles)

Moderate/ strenuous

Terrain

The route ascends some mighty, though not too lengthy, hills: Monks' Road from Charlesworth and from

Refreshments

*Several pubs, cafes and shops in **Glossop***
*Moorfield Arms, **Rowarth***
*Hare and Hounds, **Mill Brow***
Cafe at Etherow Valley Country Park
*Pubs in **Mottram in Longdendale***

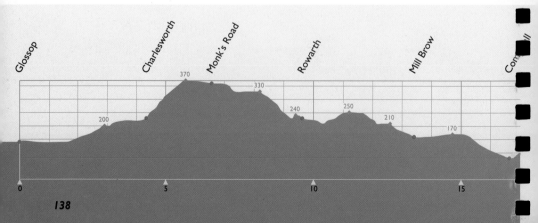

Compstall to Werneth Low. The descent of Apple Street (17–18) is also steep and will need care. Another steep rise to cross the River Etherow between Broadbottom and Charlesworth, however, there are long stretches of more gentle descent

Nearest railway

Broadbottom, Dinting, Glossop and Marple

Places of interest

Compstall 10
A former mill village. Nearby Etherow Country Park stretches north for about a kilometre along both wooded banks of the Etherow from the mill pool. The park has much of interest in natural history and there are several trails to walk

Werneth Low 13
The obelisk and the surrounding land form the War Memorial of the former Borough of Hyde. There are panoramic views in almost all directions, across the Cheshire Plain into Wales, as well as towards the Peak and Pennines. Facilities include a visitor centre and cafe, open at weekends

Mottram 18
The artist LS Lowry lived here. There is a conservation area, and a prominent maypole-like structure at the crossing into Church Row

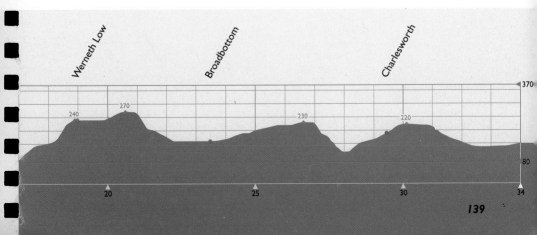

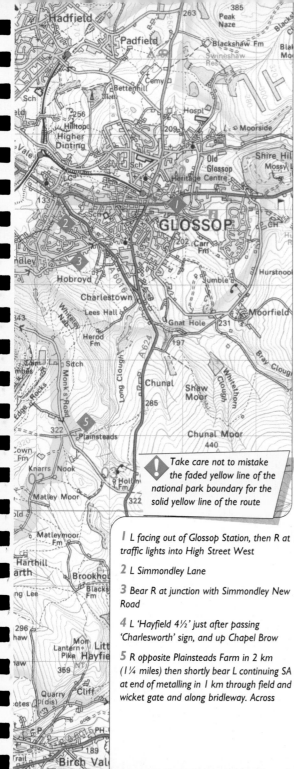

miniature ford and uphill (**not** L through gate along footpath) to second wicket gate, where L along farm drive into Rowarth and SA, passing car park on left

6 R at T-j 'New Mills'

7 L at T-j 'New Mills', then immediately R (with Moorfield Arms PH on your left) and continue for 3 km (2 miles) always bearing R

8 R at T-j with A626, then immediately L Cote Green Road

9 R at T-j Cote Green Lane

10 R at T-j with B6104 (NS)

11 Drop to crossing of River Etherow, then climb for 1 km

12 R Coulishaw Lane (NS) at triangular junction at brow of hill, then bear R in 2 km (1¼ mile) at further triangular junction at top of hill (**take care** – busy road)

13 L, then immediately R and bear R again into Werneth Low Road at off-set X-roads (in effect SA and follow road markings)

14 Bear R (steak house ahead) past 'Unsuitable for Motors' sign and down steep, concrete-surfaced track (**take care** – there are transverse drainage channels and a tight LH bend on the steep section)

15 R at T-j with Mottram Old Road

16 2nd L Chapman Road, then R at T-j Hattersley Road East

17 R at T-j, then SA at X-roads (traffic lights) into Ashworth Lane

18 SA into Church Brow at X-roads in Mottram-in-Longdendale

19 L at T-j, then under railway bridge into Lower Market Street, cross River Etherow and bear R uphill on Long Lane

20 L at T-j in Charlesworth, then immediately R into Town Lane '3 tonne limit' bearing L into High Lane 'Simmondley 1, Glossop 2'. Follow High Lane, bearing L where it becomes Simmondley Lane, returning to Glossop Station by reverse of outward route

! Take care not to mistake the faded yellow line of the national park boundary for the solid yellow line of the route

1 L facing out of Glossop Station, then R at traffic lights into High Street West

2 L Simmondley Lane

3 Bear R at junction with Simmondley New Road

4 L 'Hayfield 4½' just after passing 'Charlesworth' sign, and up Chapel Brow

5 R opposite Plainsteads Farm in 2 km (1¼ miles) then shortly bear L continuing SA at end of metalling in 1 km through field and wicket gate and along bridleway. Across

Cycle Cycle Cycle
TOURS TOURS TOURS

The Ordnance Survey Cycle Tours series

Around Birmingham
Around London
Avon, Somerset & Wiltshire
Berks, Bucks & Oxfordshire
Cornwall & Devon
Cumbria & the Lakes
Dorset, Hampshire & Isle of Wight
East Anglia – South
Gloucestershire and Hereford & Worcester
Kent, Surrey & Sussex
Peak District
Southern Scotland
South, West and Mid-Wales
Yorkshire Dales

*T*he whole series is available from all good bookshops or by mail order direct from the publisher. Payment can be made by credit card or cheque/postal order in the following ways

By phone

Phone through your order on our special *Credit Card Hotline* on *01933 414000*. Speak to our customer service team during office hours (9am to 5pm) or leave a message on the answer machine, quoting your full credit card number plus expiry date, your full name and address and reference T606N732

By post

Simply fill out the order form opposite and send it to:
Cash Sales Department, Reed Book Services, PO Box 5, Rushden, Northants, NN10 6YX

Cycle Cycle Cycle
TOURS TOURS TOURS

I wish to order the following titles

Title	Price	Quantity	Total
Around Birmingham ISBN 0 600 58623 5	£9.99		
Around London ISBN 0 600 58845 9	£9.99		
Avon, Somerset & Wiltshire ISBN 0 600 58664 2	£9.99		
Berks, Bucks & Oxfordshire ISBN 0 600 58156 X	£9.99		
Cornwall & Devon ISBN 0 600 58124 1	£9.99		
Cumbria & the Lakes ISBN 0 600 58126 8	£9.99		
Dorset, Hampshire & Isle of Wight ISBN 0 600 58667 7	£9.99		
East Anglia – South ISBN 0 600 58125 X	£9.99		
Gloucestershire and Hereford & Worcester ISBN 0 600 58665 0	£9.99		
Kent, Surrey & Sussex ISBN 0 600 58666 9	£9.99		
Peak District ISBN 0 600 58889 0	£9.99		
Southern Scotland ISBN 0 600 58624 3	£9.99		
South, West and Mid-Wales ISBN 0 600 58846 7	£9.99		
Yorkshire Dales ISBN 0 600 58847 5	£9.99		

Postage and packing free

Grand total

Name_____ (block capitals)

Address _____
_____ Postcode

I enclose a cheque/postal order for £ [   ] made payable to **Reed Book Services Ltd**

or please debit my ☐ Access ☐ Visa ☐ American Express ☐ Diners account

number ☐☐☐☐ ☐☐☐☐ ☐☐☐☐ ☐☐☐☐

by £ [   ] expiry date ☐☐ ☐☐ _____ Signature

• **Free postage and packing** • Whilst every effort is made to keep prices low, the publisher reserves the right to increase prices at short notice. • Your order will be despatched within 28 days, subject to availability
• Registered office: Michelin House, 81 Fulham Road, London SW3 6RB. Registered in England No 1974080